The Race to Eternity

The Race to Eternity

With Eternal Consequences

Diane Freeman

Library of Congress Control Number:		2017908366
ISBN:	Hardcover	978-1-5434-2661-8
	Softcover	978-1-5434-2660-1
	eBook	978-1-5434-2659-5

Print information available on the last page.

Rev. date: 09/25/2019

To order additional copies of this book, contact:
Xlibris
1-888-795-4274
www.Xlibris.com
Orders@Xlibris.com
759823

To the God Most High whose
name is to be lifted up above all
other names in Heaven, and on
Earth, for there are none like Him,
nor shall there ever be.

To Him, the Host of Heaven,
and of Earth, to Him be the glory.

Diane Freeman

FOREWORD

In the image on the front cover you see two reindeer in a confrontation with one another. They are struggling, fighting for territory or dominance in their region. Life is a similar struggle for many reasons. Evil exists on this plane in which we live. Sometimes you come face to face with it depending on what you choose to do with yourself and your free will here. So we can experience that sometimes directly or by the choices we make or by the people we meet who have chosen to entertain evil and let it rule over them. It is time to make our choice whether we are for good or for evil but even then you surely will struggle or fight against evil as it exists in this world.

It is sad but sometimes the battling between horned animals such as the reindeer causes them to lock horns and neither can extract themselves from the entanglement and they eventually do fall over exhausted and unable to eat or drink and they do die...stuck together. There is symbolism here too for mankind. If you entangle yourself with evil but do not extract yourself from it before death your demise is dark indeed. You remain stuck with the evil you have entertained. Those whom I have helped have described this scenario to me when I assisted them in crossing to freedom.

Fortunately for those I have assisted after death, the "game administrator" of life if you will, allowed them to come out of the matrix of darkness and return to their higher selves who they are when they are not in the game. When given the opportunity most souls do prefer good to evil having experienced it firsthand when they otherwise don't make any choice and find themselves surrounded by dark entities and darkness.

Let me try to explain this in a simpler way. The "darkness" is as though you were involved playing an intense, life like video game and someone kills your character in the video game but you, the human playing the game, never get your consciousness back and you are stuck in this game reality believing the lie that you have to stay there. Your humanity is attached to this idea that you cannot go anywhere too because "the greater self", that which is the fullness of you as a being, is into the video game 100%.

Unfortunately, if you don't leave the game upon completion, there are those who are in the darkness who are choosing evil who will make you miserable because you are there with the realization of what has happened and that you have no escape.

Life is a struggle not to end up "stuck". The reindeer tell a bit of this story by their predicament. Without someone coming along to assist them, they will die.

Most of you know the animal kingdom is fighting for their very survival too. Not just within their own ranks of species but due to humanity's desire to have trophies of animals particularly the reindeer, elk, and deer horns which are magnificent but they are not ornaments for mankind but potential life when a battle comes their way to the animals who have them. There is this and then there is the destruction of habitats and environments throughout the entire world which is destroying waterways, natural food sources for animals and protective hideaways for animals. Finally, there is simply the programming that has been imbedded in mankind that teaches that we need to eat animals to live and that the killing of some of them is a great sport. We have much to learn.

It is time for mankind to wake up to their nature and to the nature of other species around them for some are good and some are bad.

Let's see if I can help with The Race to Eternity.

The Race to Eternity

Is it real? I have the proof and it is within the pages of this book as real life encounters with those who have died only to become trapped in perpetuity as it were, share their stories of what they saw, what they felt and what pulled them out of darkness.

The *Race to Eternity* will uncover the truth behind what happens at death and what occurs to the soul of the individual whose life is entangled with the energies of emotion of this world. The *Race to Eternity* will detail for you, personal experiences of the author, Diane Freeman, as she was guided to assist certain individuals in their transition from life to eternity but who had been waylaid by their experiences of life. They had become entangled in the energies of the planet and were unable to move forward as is intended for all people of the planet having the experience of life in a body. Let Diane Freeman bring understanding to all of you who wish to understand the meaning of life in the body and what happens to the soul at death for no man knows the hour of his death and death happens to us all, in the body that is, for the soul lives eternally. Let *The Race to Eternity* assure you that your soul has the understanding that it needs to move on when the time comes. So be it.

Contents

Chapter One

State of the Mind

What is the state of the mind in the average individual? What is it that is being expressed in the mind of individuals on a day to day basis anyway? Is there a beginning or an end to what man can think in a day's time, or is one limited to how much they can think or how much they can process in 24 hours time? I am here to tell you that there is *no* limit to the capacity of the mind to think for it is conceived of in spirit, or energy form, and exists in time and space as physical yet its capacity to think is limitless.

This may be hard for you to grasp particularly if you are not accustomed to thinking that the body is connected by energy to a greater essence of life which exists as spirit. Now the use of the term "spirit" for purposes of this book shall mean the following: spirit is the true essence of man, which exists outside of time and space but which is accessible to man at any time, not being limited by anything but the man himself. Some of the things which do, however, limit man in his ability to connect to his higher self are the following: blockages in his etheric energy biofield, mental attitudes about his nature, lack of understanding of the ability of man to be more than just a body, emotional or physical limitations which define the person as "such and such" incapable of doing more than what has already been outlined for them by the medical or psychological establishments of this world, and finally; blockages within the body itself which cause undue stress to the individual when attempting to connect to his higher self.

We will discuss in this book how one can eliminate these blockages whether they are emotional or physical to allow mankind to reconnect with his higher being.

This will enable the population to have an encounter of his most utmost excellence in nature, the meeting of the higher self. No other experience equals this reconnection of man with his higher nature for this connection was intended to be established during the experience of life, within this planet, but unfortunately it has been lost for generation upon generation partially due to programming from the world. This programming does not allow mankind to realize who he is, and in part due to the reluctance of mankind to seek knowledge of his true identity. Though it is never hidden by the Source itself, it is hidden by other men who wish to control the minds and hearts of mankind in order to thwart them in their accomplishing all that they are here to accomplish.

Let there be a bit of understanding at this point in this narration for one must understand something about himself before he can rationally interpret the scenes around him in the world.

You are not alone in this world. There are others here as well who do not share your nature. Theirs is quite different than your own and yet if you are not capable of controlling your energy in the body, or in the mind, they will do it for you. It is as simple as that. Does this surprise you? It should not. Why would a world so incredibly beautiful and prosperous be inhabited by only one nature? Is it possible that you have lived your life with your head in the sand to prevent you from thinking of such possibilities out of fear? If so, you have played right into the hands of those who wish to keep themselves hidden for to reveal themselves would be to lose power and authority over the rest of you.

Now no man would serve another entity whose only desire is to control and manipulate you if you had another choice, correct? Most of mankind wishes to have autonomy of one another. The choice to have freedom and liberty is widespread in this world and this is the truth. So what do you say to the idea that you are not alone in this world and that your thoughts have been controlled and manipulated in many ways since the beginning of time? Does this bother you? If so why? Is it because you do desire your autonomy of such controllers? This is important to establish for there are those whose being does not exist in time and space who watch over the affairs of men who wish to honor our desires for freedom if this is what we truly desire. Is it? You must decide.

Now take a moment to think about this. As you are thinking, be aware of your thoughts. Are you hearing negative, controlling and manipulative comments about the thought of being free? If so, this is the mindset of the world contradicting your true desires and even the thought of it.

How did this controlling and contradictory thought pattern come to be imbedded in the minds of men? Good question. I am glad that you asked. This took some ingenuity on the parts of those whose desire was to control mankind. How do you control a people whose innate desire is to be remain free to make personal choices and to have creative ideas of their own? How do you get into the minds of men to manipulate thought?

It is easy enough if you know how to do it. First, you need a medium in which many people will become entranced while watching action and hearing sound. This is simple Hypnotism 101. Create a diversion while the controllers manipulate the minds from beyond the screen without the knowledge of those watching or listening. This scheme was discovered back in the 60's and 70's and exposed, but once exposed, people seemed to lose interest in the fact that this was happening to them and once again became entranced in the medium of television and movies, happily eating their snacks of popcorn and chips while sipping Coca Cola. Little did they know, the very snacks they choose are being chosen due to subtle sublimination going on behind the scenes appearing on the television or computer screen. Is this wrong?

We think so, and We are the authors of Creation who present this information to you here, for it is Our desire that all men remain free. In order to have the experience of life intended for you to have here, you must remain free. Anything else is slavery, regardless of race, creed or color. Without free choice, you are mere slaves of another who is controlling you for a personal or corporate objective. There is no other explanation for when one loses his freedom, he becomes subject to the whims of others, being manipulated and controlled without choice for what he will do with his life, his money, his children, his property, his inheritance, his body before, and even after death. It no longer becomes his right to choose anything for himself, for he has given that right to those who control him. Is this what you want for yourselves in the world today?

This was never the intention of the Creator of this world and its' people, that they would be subjects of another for the duration of their lives on the earth. It makes for a boring and unsatisfying existence, dare We say?

This being the case, your eyes are being opened to the truth such that you will take your thoughts captive and liberate your minds once again. You must know who it is that is doing the thinking within your brain. Is it *you*? How do you know? There are enough programmed messages *out there* at the moment to overwhelm the best of you. You must exercise your brain by asking yourself these questions. What am I thinking? Why am I thinking it? Do I wish to think this? If not, cast that thought off, or better yet, use your power to send it to the light where it is reformulated, hopefully into a better, less controlling thought the next time that this energy is used.

This is the way the brain was meant to function, entertaining thought from those on the planet, but then making a personal decision as to whether to believe the thought or to let it go. A person can believe the thought without embracing it and allowing the thought to remain within one's dynamic energy field, for this merely uses up the energy contained there for creating your own thoughts.

It is always better to consider that which you hear, and then, let it go. You need not keep the thought to have it only replay itself within your energy field, and mind, over and over again, like a broken record, making it impossible to consider any other thought. Here is your freedom.

Take your thoughts captive again, and know where they are coming from. If you don't like what you hear, say so. This also is part of the experience here, to know how it is that different men and women think about a thing. We are not all created the same when it comes to what a man thinks. But all are created the same in that we are able to consider the thoughts of others, and embrace them, or let them go, not wanting them to become a part of us. It is always better to remain neutral, until such time that you are required to choose one way or the other concerning a matter and this way your energy is not consumed by other people's thoughts, or worse; by controlling thought created by The Elite who manipulate such things.

Who are The Elite? We will discuss this later in this book but for now, suffice it to say, they are not your friends, for they desire to use you for their own purposes in having the best of everything available in life, for themselves, their families, their partners and no one else. Do not kid yourself that they are interested in you beyond this truth. They will take whatever they need to take so that they can live at the top of the hill with all of the money, your money, in many instances and you will not find them slaving away at 60 hours per week in hard labor. Not these people, for they have discovered an easier way to make money off the backs of men. There will be more on this later. Let us focus for now on how we must understand the nature of thought if we are to eradicate all controlling thought which originates from outside of ourselves from our minds. If we are to become free thinkers again, this truth is essential to getting there.

The mind is a powerful thing indeed but most people are not using it as a powerful thing for there is too much mind control going on in our midst. Despite our ability to want to discern such things, it is happening, to all of us. The first thing to do is to recapture your own thoughts as previously mentioned. Discover the origin of your own thoughts. Then, look around. Who is attempting to control your thoughts? Watch the way in which people speak to you. Do some people nod their heads up and down as they talk to you as if to say to you, "you agree with me, you agree with me"? Watch them. You will see it. This is manipulation.

Do some people smile at the end of each sentence they are saying to you while trying to sell you something? Again, they are trying to sell you something, they must appear friendly. This too is manipulation. Do you hear people throughout their speeches using voice inflection in order to convince you of "the truth"? If it is the truth, you do not need their fancy way of speaking to take you to it. You will know what the truth is as your body should tell you. Your mind should discern it, but in order to get there again, we must clear your mind of the mantras of others, the ticker tape parade of thought patterns and controlling words which have been set in motion to control you and your movements on the planet. The fear that has been implanted in any of you who watch television is beyond criminal. Yes, fear. Fear so you will not exercise your rights to be free to move about your planet. It is proven that fearful people stay home.

Now, before moving on, let's take a test. Sit quietly for a moment here. Listen to your thoughts playing in your head. What are you hearing? Do you hear something like this? "This is impossible. This is not the truth. I disagree. I do not believe this. This is more conspiracy theory but not the truth." Listen....what did you hear? If you are hearing thoughts such as those listed above, you need to clear your mind for you are infected with spyware. Yes, spyware. The computer is not so unlike the mind is it? It is designed to function like the brain, analyzing your problems, assisting you with decisions, popping up answers to your questions, your searches, your every whim. Right there, done for you. What do you think is so hard about infecting the brain with spyware? You are being watched all of time as to what choices you do make. If those same people watching you wish to change your thought patterns, they merely install directives to the contrary of what you are doing, and hide them behind the scenes.

In order to reestablish your own mind's will and control over what thoughts you wish to embrace, you must first see the problem. Do you see it? If you can see it, it can be fixed.

Now, what the brain sees and what the brain retains are the same. Whether you actually see it in conscious thought or not is irrelevant. The brain sees it and so it is registered. This is the problem those who wish to control others are flashing symbols, words, ideas, etc. behind what you are watching all of the time. This is affecting the thoughts and decisions of humanity in the direction in which The Elite wishes to direct you. Is this satisfactory with you? Are you content with the notion that someone else is controlling you and how you spend your time, money, what type of partner you choose for life, your sexual attitudes and family patterns and morality?

Do you wish to relinquish all control over your choices for your life? If not, then it is time to wake up and realize that it is being done so what do you want done about it?

If you are desirous of having your mind back for your own purposes in selecting life choices while in this world, then keep reading. The answers are here, in this book. It is time to bring freedom back to the individual.

Chapter Two

Eradicating the Mind's Blockages

The mind is a power thing and it is capable of doing many things for you, if you know how to use it. Most people are content to let the mind use them, and therefore they are only using a very small percentage of the mind's capacity for knowledge and wisdom and creating the life that they want to live. Those who have figured it out are using much more of their brains to create a profitable life indeed, in many instances, at your expense. How you ask? It is simple. If you won't use your brain, they will. They know how to, so why not? As long as you are somewhat content in the world, there is no reason for them to allow you to reach your full capacity to be who you are and who you came here to be in the first place.

Now, we believe that you ought to be able to choose for yourself how it is that you wish to live your life and that is why We are writing this book using our channel Diane Freeman to do so. She hears Us using much more of her brain to do so than most people realize is even possible to do. Each and every human being is connected to a higher being which is also them. Sound incredible? Indeed, it is incredible, and We are very proud of Our creation which made this possible. But in order to continue to have this type of relationship between higher beings and mankind it is necessary to clear the energy biofields of man. This is necessary due to the breakdown of the energy fields of the earth which typically would support the energy of the body, but due to the creative mind of man creating that which is contributing to the breakdown of the energy biofield, We are having to make some of Our own adjustments not only in the body itself, but in Creation.

This We are doing for your benefit, however, it is absolutely going to cause some discomfort in the bodies of men. Why is this? Because the body is confounded in many ways due to toxins from the environment, toxins in the water systems, toxins in the food supply, not to mention; the toxins in medicinal products that are being consumed by the millions by the people of this planet. In order to raise the energy level of mankind, We must elevate the body's energy system to higher levels than before.

If the body is full of toxins in the cells, the energy will struggle to rebuild the body by removing the toxins first, and this can be uncomfortable, particularly if an individual continues to put the toxins back in the body while this process is continuing on.

We are going to do Our very best to rebuild the bodies of all men, but We are not responsible for those who choose to contaminate their bodies with food that is not food and drink that is poisonous to the cells. We must encourage all of you therefore, to begin to make better dietary choices so that you can receive the energy you need for life in the immediate future.

Our process of restoring the planet has begun. We are bringing up the energy of the electromagnetic fields of the earth. This will indeed serve man well if he listens to what We tell him. Changes will take place in the body as We do this. Rejuvenation is possible as the energy system is elevated. Youthfulness will be restored to the degree that the individual changes the nature of what he consumes for the body. Now what may be popular may not be what is good for the body. We are going to encourage all of mankind to reconsider the consumption of animals for food. Animals were not given to the earth for food, but rather for companionship. Animals are a unique type of energy creation and each animal type is capable of communication with mankind in his healthiest nature. Unfortunately, mankind has lost his ability to feel the communication from animals for the most part, except in rare cases when pet owners feel that their animals speak to them almost like any person would. This is due to a unique connection between the human and the animal in which the thoughts are shared energetically between the animal and the person. It is possible and We are here to tell you that it is possible. Sadly, many animals are merely raised for slaughter and so few of you are aware of the uniqueness of the animals themselves and the contribution that they can make to your existence on the planet if you were communicating with them.

We would like to see these types of relationships restored. This is how it was meant to be, but first, We must clear the energy biofields of mankind in order for them to see again who it is that they are as beings. When We complete the process of restoring the earth's atmospheric energy pulses and compositions, We will begin to work with clearing all of humanity. We must do first things first. We must restore the earth and then We can restore humanity.

Those who listen to Us, the collective consciousness of man, will find the new experiences they are able to have exciting and rewarding. Those who do not listen will be given an opportunity to accept the new dynamic paradigm or leave. It is that simple. We are no longer going to allow the destruction of life on the planet as it has been occurring for so many years now. The animal kingdom must be restored.

The trust between mankind and the animal kingdom has been eroded from years of abuse of the animals being removed from their habitats, caged, deprived of freedom to run and play in the wild, to reproduce naturally, and to enjoy life on the planet. This is wrong and cannot and will not be accepted any longer by those of Us who created the planet and who created you.

Now is the time for a new earth and We will see to it that it occurs this time. We are going to instate Our people in positions of leadership around the globe and We are going to clean things up. This may sound a bit like a threat but it is not. It is merely the truth. The truth is the truth regardless of how it sounds to those listening. If you do not like it, it is because it threatens you in some way perhaps due to your perception that you must change or adjust to adapt to the truth. So be it. Change you must for We must restore the earth to its peaceful condition in order to have life be the experience that it was created to be. We are anticipating that many here will rejoice at the news of these changes that will be implemented. However there *are* those who will not, for long have they held power and authority over the peoples of the earth and they are not likely to go down without a fight. Leave them to Us. We created them and We know what to do. Simply do what you each individually must do to adapt to the higher energies coming into the planet at this time, and allow Us to eradicate those whose ambition drives them to do that which is evil.

Now We have a plan and it is being implemented as We speak to you here. By the time many of you read this book, many of you will have been experiencing the higher levels of energy on the planet. Do not fear. You will adjust. It is essential for you and for those who inhabit the planet with you that you adjust. We can help you in the process of adjusting but you must be willing to do as We recommend.

Many of you will be unable without the assistance of a healer to clear your energy biofields of emotional baggage shall we say. These energies of emotion become entrenched in the energy biofields of men because it is easy to do so as long as the individual is not in charge of their energy, and the offending energy is not recognizable to them any more due to a damaged energy biofield. The emotional energy is content to sit within your energy field using your energy for life until such point as you recognize it for what it is, acknowledge it and send it on its way, preferably back to the light of energy source from whence it came. It takes a bit of faith to believe it since men are not yet awake enough to accept their nature as being energy while inhabiting a physical body.

The understanding of man's nature will come in due time. In the meantime, again, you must work to clear the body of chemical toxins from the food you are eating, the water you are drinking, etc. Evaluate what you are eating. Is it organic? Where did it come from? How was it treated before you purchased it for consumption? What is in it? Why are certain ingredients being put into the food or water supply? Start asking questions and then start demanding that the food and water supply be cleaned up. If you don't ask for it, it will never happen. You are paying a dear price for not asking and it shows in the numbers of early deaths among you. Some die earlier than others due to the sensitivity of their particular bodies to the poisons and toxins being added to the food or drink supply. This is highly immoral and unnecessary by those who are doing it and it is time to hold them accountable. Or are you too toxic to be motivated? If so, ask for Our help in cleaning up the body and the planet. We need to hear from you in great numbers that this is your desire. We can do it. We know how and We have the means to do it. Just ask.

Having said all of these things now, We hope that you understand that you are not alone in your quest to rejuvenate yourselves and your planet. We are here now and We are not leaving until We reinstate the proper authorities on the planet. Man was not meant to be alone.

Man was created in the image of an Almighty Creator and this relationship must be restored so that guidance for protection of one's self and this planet can be given throughout your lifetimes. If you choose to go it alone, you end up with what you have now, a declining world and world systems. This is going to be hard for those whose desire it is not to believe in a God, Creator or any other guiding force of life. They will struggle in the body just from those mindsets themselves which they refuse to let go of in spite of the reality which is shown to them. But We tell you the truth, you must embrace the truth that there is a Creator and you must let go of the denial or you will suffer greatly in the body as the higher energy elevates your energy biofield. This is due to the nature of the energy which constitutes unbelief. Unbelief is a negative energy field. If you embrace it, and it continues in your energy field supporting your ideology of unbelief, it will confound your ability to receive the higher energy coming to the planet to support life. The result could be tragic and there is nothing anyone can do to stop it unfortunately because We, the Creators, will bring about this change in order to save life on the planet. This is out of the hands of men now. We have heard the requests of many to intervene on behalf of humanity to restore life to its original intention.

Now it is Our turn to show you what We can do.

Chapter Three

Stuck in Time

There is a condition which occurs to humanity when they are in their final moments of life here on earth that is barely understood by the best of those and not understood at all by the very least. What We are discussing when We state the "very best of those", is to indicate those who have a greater understanding of the afterlife, and those who are connected to their Divine selves, without which there is little understanding about one's own self, much less what happens in the lives of others who pass from the body into eternity. We are here to bring a few things to the light you might say and We are doing it now for the purposes of all humanity. This is not being done to enhance one person's life, but all the lives of those who live on the earth. No one is exempt except in the case of those who wish to be exempted out of such "nonsense" as they would say. Let's look at the word "nonsense" itself. If something is deemed nonsense what that really means is that the truth of the matter makes "no sense" to the one looking at it. This is a true statement for many are those who are so asleep in their bodies that to embrace something that is albeit true, because they are unable to "see it", it becomes nonsense to them in their lack of understanding, and so it will remain nonsense until they are properly healed in their energy biofields to receive truth.

We state this truth for those who are quick to cry "conspiracy theory" or some other negative descriptive term to the things they do not yet grasp nor do they understand. This is the nature of man. That which he cannot comprehend he denies the truth of its existence or possibility. In this state of mind, mankind has lost much of what was coming to him through

Divine intervention for the purposes of healing the planet and the mind of man. However, such is the nature of The Divine to continue to bring forth the truth until it is received regardless of the time element involved in getting the truth there. This is the nature of love, i.e., to continue to move forward with the truth for the express purpose of bringing about a positive change in the lives of those loved. This is a common occurrence among parents who see a child go astray only to desire that they return to positive attitudes or purposes in life rather than to choose that which has negative consequences. Unfortunately, all responsibility must remain in the one to choose for themselves what they will do in order to experience life for themselves. To attempt to prevent the outcome of choices in an effort to eliminate the pain of consequences merely circumvents life as We know it to be and eventually the person becomes stale with the purpose of life as he is incapable of feeling consequences. Without consequences it is much more difficult to choose what is a good choice, and what is the bad.

So my friends, it is built into the system for this express purpose. Experience life as much as you want however you yourself will pay the consequences for your actions and no one else.

This brings Us to the subject at hand. What happens to the person at the end of their lives when they have made numerous choices which they are not particularly happy about and they now see the error of their ways and how their choices have affected the lives of others to their detriment? What happens? Does this person have the same opportunity as others to return to the homeland of heaven as it is described by those of you on earth?

Or does this person suffer in a no man's land of terror caused by a horrific fallen angel or host of beings who exist for the express purpose of torturing those who enter in there? What do you think? What have you been told? What do you believe?

Let Us put your mind at ease now with the truth. There is a holding place of sorts where souls can rest and build up their energy prior to entering into the kingdom of heaven. It was never meant to be a "hell" or a place where souls would be tormented for eons. It was meant to be a place where souls could rejuvenate from the process of life while their energy was replenished from above at a reasonable pace such that they would not be endangered from a rapid accent into the heavens. With the energy body being depleted due to elemental toxins and food and water toxins, it is necessary to rejuvenate the body prior to ascension. There are cases where an individual is already rejuvenated prior to death and in these rare cases, there is no delay prior to being reunited with the Divine self. But as We said, this is rare as the earth is in disrepair at this time and in need of a rejuvenation process itself which We are attempting to provide for life on the planet to continue. This is a job that only We can do for We are the Creators of life and We know what is necessary to rebuild the planet. Of course there are steps that mankind can take to reduce his pollution of the planet's waterways but even then, time takes its toll on the planet and rejuvenation is necessary regardless.

Mankind is in need of the ability to restore the planet's waters, animal kingdoms, food supply, and objectives for life on the planet all of which must come from Us as contact with Us has been lost for some time. Man has had his shot at making the planet viable for life and as a consequence, life is starving at best. All types of life are starving around the globe and not just from a lack of food, but from a lack of energy. We are going about fixing this problem at this moment and it will take some time to do it but do not despair. It is happening. What is not necessary is that you give away all of your freedoms to others who purport to have all of the answers to solving "global warning" and other clichés for the planet's ailments. Mankind is the one responsible for much of what is happening on the planet but they are not responsible for all of it. Some of what is happening is due to the evolution of life. Things must change in order to support a greater level of understanding of life in the body and as to how it is connected to Divine providence. We are also here to assist with this understanding and We are not leaving this time for mankind has a short memory when it comes to staying connected to his higher self. This time We will set up a kingdom hierarchy on the planet and those who rule with Us will understand the greater truths and teach others how to live by them.

This time We will not allow evil to rule the planet and to destroy what is good while eliminating the possibilities of creative life for everyone. This situation will no longer stand. We are bringing in a higher level of government than the earth has experienced in a very long time. Some of you will have recall of these times either from your studies of the earth's history or from your higher self reiterating the truth of these times for you. Either way, it is time for this hierarchy to replace what has been the established rule on the planet, for in case you have not noticed, it is not working.

All men are given equal opportunity in life to seek to achieve their greatest potential. What most people do not comprehend is the soul's desire to come into life on the planet with greater challenges to getting there. Some people choose the difficult path to attempt to rise to greatness on their own, unassisted by others, to prove that they can indeed do it regardless of the circumstances they are subject to in a family, community, country or other challenge. Others come into being who desire to have little challenge to their objectives and so the soul seeks to be born into a family of means such that they can reach their potential quickly accomplishing as much of their goals in a short period of time. Both choices are acceptable for it is the soul's desire to choose not Ours and We accommodate both choices by assisting in the selection of parents for a soul to be incarnated into being.

If a governmental entity begins to operate in such a means as to rob the individual of his personal choices than the objectives of a soul can never be met for the greater authority over them on the planet is now government and not their higher self. This is not as it was intended to be. Personal choice is superior to governmental rule by a governing body. Thus this cannot be allowed to continue for to allow it to continue is to circumvent the soul's path to enlightenment. Hence, We are bringing in a higher authority on the planet and all of humanity will recognize it for what it is and honor it accordingly. This is not an option for We must reestablish order, freedom, personal choice and the happiness of men in pursuing their own goals. In order to do so, We must reinstate the hierarchy of the Order of Melchizideck. For those of you who have never heard of the Order of Melchizideck, let Us introduce Ourselves.

We are the highest authority in the Universe of Man and as such have the ruling authority over earth, the planets within this star system as well as a number of others. We are not self appointed but selected by the Creator of all things. This is undisputed and as such authority is given to Us to resolve the problems occurring in our universes and star systems. You can well imagine that solutions to the problems occurring on earth at this time are not simple but must be well planned and executed in order to assist all in their soul's travels. We have heard from many of you as to the problems which you are incurring in your bodies and in your minds due to lack of proper food and water and due to those who are controlling such things tainting the human experience. It is upon Us to act. We have begun the process of restoring energy on the planet. Some of you have already been experiencing the physical changes coming to the body. Pains in the hands and feet that are excruciating are not uncommon. We must urge you not to medicate yourselves for these aches and pains for to do so will interfere with the energy coming in to you to support life however, if you must, consult with your doctor and then do what is in your heart to do for yourselves. But remember, We are the higher authority now and Our interests are for the whole, not for Ourselves, but for the whole of humanity that you may do well in your being so life may continue as it should for an enhanced soul experience.

Take a moment now to consider what it is that We have said to you thus far. Does it resonate with you as the truth? If not, ask yourself why? What pervasive thoughts are running through your mind at this time? Are they negative? If so, where are they coming from? Do you know? Can you take those thoughts captive? Can you quiet them? If not, why not? Are you not the master of your own mind? Have you lost the ability to control your own thoughts to the dominating thoughts or controlling mindsets of the world in which you live? Now is the time to wake up and realize that patterns of thought run through your societies in an effort to control your actions, not just what you think. A submissive population is much easier to control than one that is active and creative in its thinking about what is good for the individual and the populace. In order to have control over another it is necessary to control what a person thinks. This is done through the media, television, radio, printed materials, culture and the like. In your world as it is now, it is difficult to have an independent thought at all, wouldn't you say?

When is the last time in which you can remember thinking a thought that was not previously heard or implanted by another individual? Think about it, if you can. Do you know that it is possible to have independent thought? You need not agree with anybody if it is your choice not to do so. This is the power of true freedom, to choose for yourself what is real and what is not real. Not to have another choose for you and to dictate the reality that you must live. Each and every human being is a creator in his own right and has the ability to create his life and circumstances in a free world. This world which you have now created is no longer free but being controlled by others who are exercising their creative genius to control you. How does that feel? "Impossible!" you say. We tell you that it is the truth. You are no longer free. Your freedom has been usurped by those who know how to do such things and what you do with your lives is now subject to their input. How much money you can make and keep, where you can live, how you can live and who you can live with in many cases is now being decided by others. This is the truth and if you are privy to it, you must do your homework and you will discover that the rules are in place now to keep you in check so to speak such that you cannot take control from those in power.

This is not as it should be and We are going to undo the damage that has been done. We begin the process through a quick exercise in enlightenment. Mankind needs to know who he is and why he is here in the first place. Do you know who you are? If not, why not? Do you care or have you become indoctrinated by the world's systems such that you no longer seek greater enlightenment but are content to live life by the dictates of others who control the actions of your life done to the very words you are able to speak freely anymore. This is true and you must admit it. You are being controlled and if you think that you are free to do as you please We challenge you to go to any street corner and begin to express some controversial views about the government and see how long it takes "them" to come and arrest you for disorderly conduct or some such thing for you are no longer free my friend. The controlling factions are in place now. Do you see them?

We do and We cannot allow life on planet Earth to be destroyed by a few men who deemed themselves "Gods" who should rule over the planet and those who live here.

In order to understand what is happening today, it becomes necessary to grasp who it is that you are and the nature of your body and experience in the body. You exist in the higher realms as energy and intellect. Your desire is to expand your consciousness and being in any way possible, for to remain the same for all eternity is a remedy for a bored existence and not desirable by your souls. Such it is that the experience of sharing a body with your energy being was designed by the higher beings. It was appointed by the higher beings to allow the consciousness of souls to inhabit bodies on the planet now called earth for the express purpose of enhancing the soul's experience through life in the body. The uniqueness of the body would allow the soul to "feel" energies in motion created by other bodies through the design of the energy biofield which surrounds each body. This experience would be unique to earth and it cannot be experienced anywhere else. Such is the beauty of the earth experience and many are those who wish to come here.

At present, there are far too many souls on the planet who are stuck in the experience of earth unable to separate their Divine nature from the nature of the body and the experiences that they are having here to move on. This is particularly troubling when the body dies and the soul is unable to separate the "feelings" of the experiences they have had in the body from the energy which is their higher nature in order to move on. Now think about this. The body is organic but it is also energy yet they are separate. One can live without the other. That "one" is the soul's energy body. The organic body exists by the very nature of the soul's presence. When the soul energy leaves at death or by choice, the body dies. There is one problem with the soul's ability to leave at death however and it has been created by the doctrine of man. When a person dies, the mind is still very much intact and capable of reuniting with the higher being whose intellect is having the body experience in the first place. If the "person" who was in the body has separated himself from his Divine being, he no longer understands that there is a connection between himself and his originating soul. He no longer "gets it" that his soul and his Divine nature are one being. This complicates his ability to reunite at death with his higher being. This truth has been kept from mankind for some time now as men who rule over the minds of men tell stories which are untrue about hell and hell's fury and the devil and such things. There is no greater hell than to be separated from your "self" whether it is in the body or out of the body. Your mind will be experiencing the nothingness of "space" as it were.

The problem is that there are those who are in that space who know exactly where they are but who have overcome the sadness of it all to rule over the minds of those who don't know where they are to their advantage. What do We mean exactly? If a man dies and is angry about his death due to what he imagined his life would be and at death he is unwilling to depart the earth's plane, he is perfectly capable of remaining here, just without his body; his mind and his energy, remains on the planet. Now, the power of the mind cannot be underemphasized. The mind is capable of influencing others even when the body is no longer viable. How you ask? Simple! The mind is energy and it is eternal.

If the individual who has departed the body wishes to oppress others who are still living rather than returning to his higher self, it is possible. The problem is that if the person does not return at death it becomes increasingly more difficult to leave as the energy diminishes over time making the "person" weaker and weaker and incapable of escape. It is possible to "recharge" these souls energy from their incarnation however sometimes it is necessary to re-enlighten them as the wayward souls who have chosen to stay have been indoctrinating trapped souls on this side of life similar to the way in which living persons indoctrinate souls in the body. It seems as though little changes between life and death and yet it does when the soul returns to his higher self and shares the experiences of life with other higher beings. There is nothing like it. It is a glorious experience to have a soul return home and much rejoicing commences upon their return. This much has been told by some in the faith and it is true. However, there is much that is told which is not the truth and it is to this We speak now by bringing forth the truth.

Earth is about to be restored to her former glory. Those of you here wishing to experience this will be in awe of this day for you will live it day by day seeing the changes in not only yourself and others, but in the planet itself and what it is capable of being for you. It is a new day. Rejoice!

Chapter Four

Doors Wide Open

What if We told you that life as you know it is ending and a new beginning is upon you all? Would this cause you to panic? If so why? Since when is a new beginning a bad thing? We are hoping that you will understand that what is coming is a good thing for all of humanity including those whose situation requires a removal from society until such time as they are ready to reintegrate having learned some vital lessons about themselves and others. Right now, the doors are wide open to embrace all of humanity in the new energy of life which is settling in on the planet as We speak. This new energy is life giving and so it shall...give life. Those who receive it will experience a rejuvenation of sorts in their hearts, minds and bodies. Those who feel it but reject it will struggle to remain in their bodies for the vibration that is settling in is of a higher vibration than what you have been experiencing in this lifetime.

Regardless of what you choose to do with the energy that is coming in, it *is* coming and there is nothing that anyone person can do about it. It is required to sustain life on the planet at this time and so We are doing whatever is necessary to assist in lifting up the planet's energy. Should you require assistance with the feelings of negativity that may overwhelm you, We have placed people on the planet who can assist you with clearing these energies from the body's energy field. They are healers who work with dynamic energy and they are capable of interpreting the body's needs. We are not asking them to work for free however as no man wishes to do so and it is evident in your societies that mankind has established a work for pay system at all levels of life. There is no reason to expect a person who is gifted in healing to work for free any more than you would expect your dentist or surgeon or therapist to work without a reward for the time and energy they are giving to bring you relief of whatever kind. Those who desire to be helped without giving something to the person helping them are merely selfish and neither giving or receiving well from others but only desiring what is good. We will not help those types of people until they yield to the established protocol We are putting in place for all men, not just some.

You can be sure that We are standing by to assist anyone who is willing to yield to Our instruction on how to be free of negative emotions or feelings and We will assist those who seek Us directly however it is not an easy task to free someone from a lifetime of embracing negative emotion. We must teach the person what is necessary for life and this takes time and understanding which is not possible for all men in their blocked states of mind and body. Thus We have trained individuals to do the work who have submitted to Our teachings who are not blocked and they are able to clear people directly. This makes it possible to clear many people at a time rather than having people attempting to reach Us, hear Us, and learn from Us who do not have "ears to hear" what it is that We have to say to humanity. Why not leave it to the "experts" then who have already put in the time to learn what to do to prepare one's self for the new energy on the planet? We have trained them well and We oversee their teachings of others. You can trust them.

Who you should not trust are those who are critical of others always judging and tearing apart the truth as though it were a lie so as to keep others from achieving their freedom. You will know them by their negativity. To them, nothing is possible. To them, only their way is the right way and they cannot see past what it is that they already know to be true, not wanting to believe anything else as possible. To those who believe, all things are possible. Have you not heard this somewhere before?

Now let's move on for there is much to say to begin the healing of the planet. If you have decided that you yourself are in need of healing of the mind, body and spirit, then you must prepare the body to be cleared. The first thing to do is to rid the body of toxins. In order to receive higher energy for life, the cells must be cleansed of all toxins which have accumulated over time. These toxins are impeding the flow of energy in the cells thus making it impossible for the new energy to be received by the body. Trust Us. You will need the new energy if you are to survive in the Age of Aquarius.

As We have stated before those who do not receive this new energy will struggle to remain in the body. The new energy is not compatible with old negative emotions. Additionally, the new energy is not compatible with a diet consisting of many animal proteins for the energy in animals is different than the energy within the human body. Though you may find this difficult to "digest" so to speak, We are telling you the truth. It is time to bring about the understanding that the animals on the planet were not put here for your consumption but rather for your assistance in learning how to live in a body. They were well adapted to life on the planet prior to the introduction of man and capable of sustaining life in their packs, dens, tribes, whatever it may have been without having to consume men nor did they. It was only when humanity turned against the animal kingdom intruding upon lands where the animals roamed freely and forced them into smaller and smaller spaces did the animals turn on themselves, other animals and ultimately mankind.

This is the truth and is verifiable through Us and those who know Us. It is time to heal the animal kingdoms of the planet and it must be done along with the healing of man. Without one, the other will not occur. They must be done simultaneously. We are going to free the wild animals of the world from the zoos, from the homes of those who have enslaved them there, and from the trade market, that solicits the sale of animals for money around the world. This We are putting a stop to immediately. You will begin to see that those who have entrapped animals in cages will begin to suffer for doing so. The animals will demand their release even if it means attacking those they love. We promise you this for it is necessary to demonstrate to humanity that the imprisonment of animals is wrong and against their nature. To imprison an animal means that it can no longer roam free to hunt for proper food, shelter or companionship. It can no longer enjoy the natural habitats created for them on the planet and is threatened with extinction if left to man's ways.

We are changing the status quo immediately and freeing the world's animals. This is a good thing and so you should rejoice. Many of you have asked for the animals to be freed for you feel their anguish as they are trapped in the world's zoos not finding joy there or harmony with their own spirits. Yes, animals have spirits too. They are capable of sharing great things with mankind and We will demonstrate this to you through the introduction of the Order of Melchizedek which too, is coming. New leadership is coming to the planet and We are bringing this about as We speak to you now. You will soon meet the real leaders of this world and it shall be as it was meant to be from the beginning. All life will be restored and all meaning of life renewed. Those who are with Us on this mission to renew the planet will be ecstatic. Those who are not will have another reaction…perhaps panic.

If they cannot continue on the path of destruction of mankind's freedom what happens to them? Better not to consider staying on that path as it is one that will lead to eventual heartache for you and those you love for you will be removed from the planet until you too are healed of the desires to be destructive. It is the only way to begin the work of renewal and it is coming. In fact, in many ways, it is already here.

We have always had the doors of life open to humanity but many have chosen other paths to destruction of life, human life, animal life, personal freedom of others. This is not what was intended for the human experience on planet Earth and in order to restore life to what it was intended to be, We are reinstating the Order of Melchizedek on the planet. You are in for a ride. Those of you who have not been privy to who We are, are soon to discover who We are. Those of you who are familiar with Us, you too shall be pleasantly surprised. Life is about to be good again. Wait for it. It is coming in now. We are introducing Ourselves now in order to avoid stirring up fear in the people of this world for fear is not from Us, nor do We wish to harm anyone. This is not who We are nor is it ever who We were. If you have experienced heartache and pain and fear and war it was not because We desired it for you nor did We encourage it ever for the people of Earth. We are a peace loving kind as were you, in the beginning.

Now let Us again say that you have time now before We reinstate Our leadership on Earth to release yourselves from the negative energies which have subsequently had a hold on you. Do it now. Not to do so will only hurt you later as the stronger energies come in. To wait is a bad choice. Move ahead. Get clear. Let go of old negative memories and forgive those who need forgiving. Release them and yourselves from the experiences of the planet and let the healing begin for everyone, not just yourself. Even those who have attempted to enslave the human race need forgiveness though you may need to see who they are in order to forgive them. We can arrange that too and We will.

Look to yourselves then first. See what it is that is "bugging you", "dogging you", "debilitating you" and let it go. These negative feelings were meant to teach you about yourselves and about others. They were not meant to become a part of your nature, changing you and your energy fields for all time. If you do not relinquish these thoughts and feelings of hatred, resentment, bitterness, grief, sadness, anger, and others, you will not be able to move forward in the new energy of life for it is incompatible with these negative emotions. Get free then. A new world is headed your way. Believe it. Celebrate it and begin to anticipate it. Assist Us in bringing it in and perhaps We can speed things up a bit for many of you are tired of the old ways for surely they are not working for you and the world begs for a healing.

Chapter Five

Entering Freedom

What would it be like to live on the earth in total and complete freedom to be who it is that you came here to be accomplishing your goals with the liberty and love from others to do so? Does anyone currently on the planet even have a notion of what that would feel like? Have we lived in captivity for so long that we have lost our way and our ability to perceive freedom? Unfortunately, it is true. Freedom has been a thing of the past for those living in today's world. The freedom to live where you choose is lost due to border patrols and boundaries in the land which prohibit the movement of man. The ability to keep what you earn is lost due to governmental and private corruption extracting much of an individual's wages for personal and private gain unbeknownst to the populace at large. The ability to attend school where you would like to attend school is lost due to political control over quotas of students in schools and exorbitant tuitions being charged for the privilege of attending these same institutions. What has happened in the world is that freedom has been stolen from the people while they were approving all of the new rules and regulations over themselves without a clue as to what it would mean for their futures or their children's futures.

The loss of life for instance has been exponentially damaging to the psyche of man and yet the awakening refused to come to demonstrate that the destruction of the unborn would merely cause men to retreat into their minds in shame and guilt for what they had done to themselves for in the creation of life, man is incorporated into another being, and in the destruction of life, man kills a part of his own being. This is the truth regardless of any indoctrination to the contrary. If you take the life of another, whether it is animal or human, it is destruction of a part of your own being for all men do come from one Being, and this Being is indestructible.

Now that you have the truth, what will you do with it? Do you believe it or is some part of you denying the truth of what We just told you? If so, that part of you which denies the truth needs to be silenced for it is ego which strives to exist apart from Us. It exists in the minds of men due to the way in which man has grown apart from Us, attempting to exist without the controls of the hierarchy of heaven.

Unfortunately, in attempting to live apart from Us, mankind has destroyed much of the earthen experience almost to complete annihilation and if it were not for Our intervention, you would succeed for surely you have created the weaponry to destroy the earth's life as you know it. We can attest to that. This same weaponry will be removed from the planet and destroyed safely apart from the earth where it cannot do any more harm. We are in the process of facilitating this now and you will see this done in your lifetimes. You must agree that this in itself is a good thing for without this type of weaponry which can destroy entire cities man can live without fear that another nation can come and wipe out all that you have accomplished for yourselves elsewhere with one bomb.

What do you think so far? Sound good? We hope so for We have formulated this plan based upon man's request for an intervention from God and for the protection from evil which We must say, has run amuck in your midst through the last century. Let it be known then that the end has come for the evil that is currently at work on your planet and We are going to rule again as once before to see to it that evil does not quickly return to destroy the earthen experience. You have much to look forward to now. Rejoice! Begin to give thanks even before you see it coming for in all things you ought to give thanks. Life is precious you see. Many long to come here still and the earth is a difficult place to navigate at best in its current condition. Yet, the desire to come here and find love is beyond measure. If you are here, and you have found love, embrace that feeling above all else for it does not exist elsewhere in the way that it exists here for love can best be felt in the absence of love. If you have not felt the absence of love how do you measure it? It is difficult so it is that many desire to feel it and earth provides that opportunity even in its worst times, it can be felt. It is the thing most missed when souls depart the earth…the ability to feel the difference between love and no love at all. It is why We created earth in the first place and why We wish to maintain its power to bless souls with this feeling for all eternity. It is unmatched you see. It is well worth the ride no matter the price to man. All seek it. All desire it. So do not regret having loved and lost for it is better to have loved and lost than not to have loved at all. This is a good saying is it not?

Chapter Six
WHY THERE IS NO HELL

It is amusing to those of Us who do not inhabit a body at this time, to see how men judge one another determining who is good and who is bad based upon some earthly criteria for deciding such things and yet, it is within the nature of all of mankind to be either good or evil. How do We know? It was part of the plan that you would experience both such that you could see the difference between the two. If one lives in an environment of pure love as a matter of course then how can it be known what is evil? It is not possible for one must experience such things in order to make a determination as to which is better wouldn't you say? For example, if you were inclined to be a person who chooses to be kind and considerate to others only to have those same people respond to you in a negative, critical, uncaring and judgmental way what would be your response? Would you think that they would be nice to you if only they could understand that you meant them no harm? What if they understand perfectly that you meant them no harm but their nature is not like yours at all? What if their nature is one to control others, hurt others, to use others for their own purposes and to eliminate you all together?

Now this is something completely different from the nature of love wouldn't you say? There is no comparison between the two. One seeks to embrace the other in love. The other seeks only to consume the other in total anarchy controlling and using those who are good for their own good pleasure. There will be no reward for being good therefore because not only is it *not known* by those who do evil, but it is *not* a part of the being of those who exhibit these behaviors of control. They cannot know it for it is not who they are.

Now what if you were told that in order to know the difference between good and evil this environment was created for that very experience and as you succumbed to the more evil influences in your environment, you became less good hence more evil? This was not the intention of the experiment or experience, you decide but that you would know the difference between one nature and the other by experiencing both at the same time. The hope was that having experienced the more controlling, manipulative and evil nature of those among you, you would desire that which is good by nature, particularly since it was who you were. Apparently the experiment has gone awry. Something has happened and the ability to perceive the difference between what is good and what is evil has been lost through the centuries. In order to repair the damage done to the psyche of man which has damaged this innate ability it will take a Divine act of healing the planet's electromagnetic fields thus healing the minds and bodies of mankind.

Now that you know that it was intentional that evil would exist among you, how do you feel? Does this upset you? Why? Do you wonder why God would want bad things to happen to good people? What if We told you that the decision to come here was your own? What if who you are and the experiences that you would have here were predetermined before your life began in the body by your own design for the very purpose of educating you about yourself, your potential as a being, and your greater understanding of other beings like yourself? How do you feel knowing this? Is it a problem for you? If so why? If you are indeed a higher being having a body experience why not experience all that there is to experience in life? Even death of the body? The problem comes when you forget who it is that you are and death comes.

Without an understanding that all men are capable of having eternal life beyond life in the body, men become trapped energetically in the state of mind of the body. Now if ever there was a "hell", that would be it. To be without a body but to left outside of the connection to your higher self. This existence would be hell. There would be no body (nobody) to help you to feel anything for no one else there would have a body either, correct? You could perceive the thoughts of others because you would still possess your energy bodies which can pick up the thoughts of others but you would not be able to communicate with the living and, in addition, not being connected to your higher self means that you become weaker in energy every day that you exist apart from your higher self.

At least in the body, the higher self is able to regenerate the body at will once a person is connected and in tune with his eternal body. Without the body, the energy is adrift. This is so for several reasons. There are those on the planet who have set in motion means by which to keep individuals from reconnecting from their higher selves. This means that as an individual dies in the body, their energy would become trapped as it were in limbo. The purpose for doing this is simple if you are attempting to control others. Knowing that it is still possible to communicate with these souls by impression of thought, there are those who manipulate the "dead" by speaking controlling thoughts over them similar to what is done through the process of sublimination which has occurred quite frequently unfortunately through the use of hidden words in television programming, and in movies, and the like.

As long as the person's soul is held captive, they cannot reconnect to their higher selves nor can they receive the energy they need to be released to the heavens and be reconnected. Now imagine what you could do with the souls of people who have left the body, who do not understand who they are or the process of reuniting with their higher selves, who are trapped energetically in the earth plane? These souls cannot be seen by the average living person and those who do see them are primarily children. When a child sees the energy of the souls who have died, they are typically told by their parents or other uninformed adults that what they are seeing is not real. Yet the child is seeing something or why would they simply make it up out of nothing? This happens for several reasons. The adult does not understand the death process. The adult has never seen the energy of someone who has passed themselves. The adult is afraid of what the child might be seeing. The adult cannot explain himself to the child what it is that they are seeing so it is better to state that they must be imaging it. This is disrespectful to the child who may not understand what it is not to tell the truth. This is also dishonoring of the abilities of the child to perceive that which is not living in the body as you know it.

A child may retreat into themselves when they are treated with this little respect for their abilities to see as they were created to see. They may hide their abilities from those who judged and criticized them and become recluse wanting to be who they are but afraid of the chastisement from others. It is far better to ask quietly what it is that the child is seeing and to attempt to determine the cause of it. Why is the child seeing that particular person's energy who has passed? Is it because they are a deceased relative who is seeking understanding of what to do themselves to move on? If so, and you can determine that it is a relative, send them home to the light indicating that all can go home. We are not here to be judged but to have an experience that we may know good from evil.

Children are keen to see spirits of the departed. They are unprejudiced in their thinking and pure in their hearts. The departed souls know this and will attempt to be seen by children in an effort to be helped in the afterlife. These souls are helpless and do not understand why they do not have a body anymore yet they are nowhere. If they have met the dark lords of the afterworld they are afraid, sad, tormented and wish to be free. Do you blame them for coming to the children for help? Particularly when the adults pretend not to see them because they too are afraid and do not know what to do with what they see?

This is the situation we are confronted with on the earth at this time. There are departed souls roaming the earth with no destination in mind. They do not know where to go or how to get there. What do you think ought to be done? Should they be helped? Are they not the mothers and fathers of many on the planet today? Is there an evil so great that any man or woman should be destined to spend eternity in a dark, empty space with no contact with anyone? Who are you to judge those who should be confined in such a way? It is not given to us as humans to judge other humans for eternity. Those who do will suffer the same consequence you can be sure for their minds have embraced the idea that it even exists and when the time comes for them to leave, they will remember that they have judged and it will prevent them from going home themselves. I promise you this for all men seem to remember at death's door that it is wrong to judge another man's eternity.

Our hope is that men will awaken to their true identity and assist Us in releasing the souls of trapped men and women and children whose eternity hangs in the balance as the energy of the earth changes for life to continue to exist on the balance. As the energy of the planet is raised, the souls who are trapped will be further debilitated and eventually it will be impossible to retrieve them. Do you see the problem now? Perhaps if you are beginning to see the problem you can understand Our attempt to reach many of you with the truth so that these souls could return to the energy of their higher selves being reunited for eternity with that which is good having had an earthen experience, good or bad, but the energy will tell the tale of what it is like to live in an environment where both good and evil exist side by side. Hopefully good triumphs and the experience can continue for all beings choosing to have it. This is the plan but it will require Divine intervention as evil has gotten quite the foothold on planet Earth. Do not dismay however for We, the Creators of all that you see and now have a handle on the situation. We know what We are doing.

First, We must educate you on who you are and why you came here and how it is that there is no hell for any human being because to condemn one would be to condemn all of you for there is not one good among you. Your thoughts tell the truth. What you think is perceived by all of Us who do not live in space and time as you do. How does that make you feel? Betrayed? Vulnerable? Indeed, We do not intervene in your thoughts unless you invite Us to do so as when you connect with your higher selves seeking guidance and direction. At this time, correction is forthcoming to you, then and only then, for to interfere with the earthen experience that a soul is having is a violation of the agreement which that soul has with the higher beings creating the experience. No interference unless it is asked for from the soul. Surprised? Now you can answer the question as to why bad things happen to good people.

There is no substitute for the understanding which comes to a soul having experienced a situation firsthand on the earth. No one else's telling of a thing can replace a person actually experiencing something for themselves and so it is that mankind wants to experience things whether it is the climbing of Mt. Rushmore, or Mt. Everest, or the swimming of the English Channel. It is the choice of the soul what his life will be like on earth and so it is not to be interfered with by Us unless of course you ask for assistance. Remember that it is said somewhere, "Ask and it shall be given". This is a true saying. It was written as a reminder to those of you here having the experience that you need only ask for direction and it will come to you. Now remember in the reading of this that you must persevere in the asking for many of you have stipulated that you do not want help on the earth plane unless the situation reaches a certain degree of hardship and no less. Your requests will be honored to the degree that you have stipulated prior to coming to earth. Why would We interfere with what you yourself asked for? This is not who We are. We are honorable, truthful, and respectful of the human condition and desiring that all men experience life as they desire to experience it. This is for many reasons. Many of you wish to test your own resolve as beings. What would you do if you were born with legs, arms, or your vision? What if you were to encounter a disease which was debilitating to your entire being and all you had left was your mind? How would you communicate with others then in a body? These and other scenarios are designed by you for you are a creative being as such and capable of many opportunities for the soul to experience while in a body. Your sympathy for others is admirable and yet you do not understand that the mature soul will remember that they chose to have the very experience that they are having and it was predetermined before birth that they would have it. Situations are set up therefore on the planet for them to have the experience which they desire to teach the soul what it is that they wish to know about themselves or others by living in the body in such a way. Now many of you may challenge this truth but in the end, it is the truth and so you merely waste time not believing it.

Now if you can, imagine that there are some rather wicked individuals among you who do not deserve life in heaven nor do they deserve sympathy or consideration for their souls. You must consider this. You are judging others and you do not know the whole truth of the creation of the earthen experience. In order for some souls to have the experience in the body which they desired to test their will, their resolve as souls, evil was created. What better way was there for souls to learn the lessons of love? One must experience love in the absence of love to determine its value. Isn't this always the case? You never know what you have until it is no longer available to you. This is the certainly the case with love. Souls are willing to put themselves to the test to determine their own measure and ability to love others. This is of great value to the soul's being. How much can you take from another and still love them? How deep is your love for them? Souls wish to test this in themselves and it is not for others to intervene and interrupt the process for to do so is to circumvent the knowledge that is gained otherwise by those having the experience. Many of you wish to rush in with abundant love wanting to "fix it" but this is not desired by the soul's being.

Therefore let people experience life as they have set out to experience it, learning by their mistakes what is love and what is not. They will learn it one way or another for this purpose they came and it was their choice, not yours, to experiment with love. This is the most difficult thing to accept for loving parents who wish to protect their children from the sadness of lost love and yet, this is how their children learn to be better lovers of humanity in general. They must love and experience loss to know what love is. The purpose in discussing all of this is to create an understanding of the purpose of life and once one understands the purpose of life it is more easily understood why it is essential not to judge the lives of others for each has chosen his own path in life and the experiences he wished to encounter for reasons of his own choosing. Can you then understand why it is not given to you or anyone else to judge whether a person should go to hell or not go to hell? Not only that, it is not given to you to decide to send a spirit or other being to hell either, for in order to have the experiences required to teach your soul survival or some other such thing certain creatures were necessary for the experience to occur whether they were living, or not living.

Let Us give you a perfect example which was given to the channel for Our book to experience for purposes of discussion. We asked her to assist another living person whose parents had died in determining whether they had crossed over. Her friend needed to know if her parents were on the right side of Heaven and whether they were together. She also asked Our channel to inquire of her parents as to why they had mistreated her and why they had not expressed or shown her love. This person needed to know these things for she had herself much anger towards her parents and it was continuing to impact her life and choices in life for she was unable to reconcile herself to the way in which she was treated by those she loved.

Our channel then went into meditation seeking the answers which her friend needed and to then assist her parents in moving on. Our channel was able to connect with the parents individually and to ask each of them the questions that her friend needed to know. What she heard was fascinating to her. Her father was not equipped he said to deal with a child who was so spiritual and who asked many questions about the world which she was living in. He did not know what to do with her. He was uncomfortable with her knowledge of things spiritual and her capacity to perceive things he could not see. He loved her but did not show her and so he apologized to her through Our channel asking for forgiveness for not telling her that he loved her and cherished her as his daughter. Similarly, her mother indicated that she was jealous of her daughter's beauty and wished that she too were beautiful.

Thus, she treated her daughter with little regard and very little love. However, as Our channel discussed the situation of pain that the woman's daughter was now living in while in the body due to the lack of parental love and kindness, both parents then felt sadness and guilt and asked for their daughter to forgive them. They both indicated that they had indeed loved their daughter but in their own feelings of inadequacy they neglected to share their love with her and in fact, exhibited something quite different. However, in the telling of the truth to their living daughter, she was able to understand why it was that her parents had treated her that way and she forgave them. Thus, she could live without the anger they had made her feel towards them in life and even, beyond their deaths. At this point, it is now up to the living to move on leaving behind the feelings of the past in order to be free of these feelings that entrap our energy beings.

Emotions are made to be felt and let go. The memory of the feeling will remain but the energy which creates the feeling in the first place must be released in order for mankind to be free to feel new emotions. This is how it was designed to be in the body. The energy created by encountering situations in the world would generate feelings in those who participated in the experience. These feelings could then be weighed against the person's experiences thus far or their memory and understanding and a determination made as to whether the experience was a good one or a bad one. Indeed sometimes the point is not even whether the experience turns out good or bad but the important thing is that the experience be had in the first place for the soul desired it and so it was that it was arranged to happen.

For all men participate in the creation of the experiences occurring on the earth plane for thought is a powerful thing. What a person is thinking is being made manifest perhaps not exactly as you might see it or like it, but it is being made manifest. The beauty of life is that not all things can be anticipated exactly as one thinks it. Creation has a bit of a mind of its own too. Remember that. In a sense, it is almost like a safety valve to protect mankind from themselves and what it is that they might imagine or think which is not perhaps the best thing for them.

Think of it this way. Would you take a young child and drop them off in a faraway country without any provision for life, with no contact with you being possible and no means of life? This is absurd and We are no different. We do not send the uninitiated into situations which have not been agreed upon prior to the situation by both the soul and the Divine leaders. All things must be done in order always. We are about having the best outcome for all humanity through the experience of life on earth. When the situation gets out of control, as it has currently, We must step in and take authority over the situation until such time as We can step away again and allow the experience to continue uninterrupted.

Unfortunately, We are at a place in time when it has become necessary to remove evil for a season of healing on the planet for much has occurred without the ability for mankind to choose the experience that he is otherwise having. Drugs, governmental influences, gangs, and electromagnetic manipulation on the planet are interfering with man's ability to choose his experiences on his own without input from others without their permission. This is why We have come to intervene at this time. This is why We will rule on the planet for a season of time to heal the minds and spirits of many of you here so that the experience of life may continue uninterrupted when We are through with Our plan of healing throughout the earth.

So now is a time to rejoice for the heartfelt prayers of many have been heard and help is on the way. The planet will receive its own clearing. The people will receive new energy, new insight about themselves and rejuvenation through Our efforts. Some of the restraints put upon mankind by those who have usurped your authority and power will be removed so that you can again enjoy the fruits of your own labors.

No man wants to work hard only to have his hard work earnings go to someone else and not his own family. This is hypocrisy and will not be tolerated any longer. Choice will be returned to the individual. You may bless those you wish with your own monies. This is as it should be and We will see to it.

So again, let Us remind you. There is no place called hell per se but only the place where a soul is now entrapped by the energy changes taking place on the planet that entrap a soul who will not release the negative emotions of life experienced while living in the body. Thus, do not wish that someone would go there for no man would desire this experience for himself much less for another were he to experience it firsthand. This kind of thinking is not love but its' opposite, hatred, and this is not of God nor is it from the natural human nature but something else created for the experience of knowing one kind from another. Thus, it must be released in order for mankind to return to his natural state of being when not in the body and this is what you must realize and embrace and tell those whom you might encounter who have passed on from life only to become entrapped in the spirit realm not knowing where to go. Now is the time for all men to come to the aid of their people, not just their country. Come to the aid of those you love and have loved who have passed on. In this way, many will be set free from the entrapment set up by others who are not human to keep Divine beings from returning to their higher selves. This is first.

Chapter Seven

WHO KNOWS THE TRUTH

What is the truth? Who can tell the world the truth in this day and time and how can one know that it is the truth even when it comes down from the highest source of truth? There is a way that seems right to a man but in the end is only death. This is a true saying certainly for many a man or woman have ended up not knowing who they were or where they were going at the end of their days in the body so for them the answer was not given to them leaving them to experience whatever was coming without the foreknowledge which would have prepared them for eternity. Hence, it is time to hear the truth and for those who hear it to embrace it for the truth is the truth regardless of who wishes to state otherwise.

The truth will resonate within those who are searching for it for it has a sound unlike any other word. The truth carries its own vibration and within the vibration of truth is the satisfaction that what one has just read, or heard, there is legitimacy. The nations are ready for the truth. There has been quite enough of tale telling and so it is that the vibration of truth will resound on the earth from end to end until all have heard it recognizing it and embracing it for themselves and others. Thus, the truth shall change the vibration of man just by the hearing of it. It will alter the destinies of men. The truth will shift the planet's course and set things in order as it should be.

So there is no need to worry anymore about what the truth is for it is coming forth as We speak to you now. As it seeps into your being, it is your very soul that will resonate with its vibration. This shall be your confirmation of its validity. You will not need anything more We assure you. There is only one truth when it comes to such matters as the nature of man and his reason for being in the body. All other tales are merely this…tales.

So take the time to allow the words you are reading to resonate with your being and then ask yourself, "what is the truth of my being?", and then wait for the answer to come. There is no one better to confirm the truth than your higher self, who is sharing the experience of life with you at this very moment of revelation of your being.

Rejoice then as your eyes are opened in the presence of the truth. Give thanks to the God of heaven for you have awakened to your true Being and know that I AM with you always.

Chapter Eight

What Can You do To Prepare For Eternity?

Much is done within the realms of earth to prepare others for one's eventual death in order that those we leave behind will inherit the labors of our work to assist in their well being when we depart the earth. This is a kindness which is extended to those we love for it is necessary for those who work to assist those who stay home taking care of the homestead and personal matters of a home so that those who work outside the home can achieve their destinies through a chosen professional. It is a fair exchange is it not? We do believe that it is indeed a fair exchange and so it is that we have sanctioned the giving of one's life achievements in property or money or personal items to the family members who are left behind. This is one way in which you can begin to prepare for eternity. Make certain that provisions have been made to allow that which you have to be transferred to those you are leaving behind at the time of your death according to your will and testament. Many are those who are helped exponentially by the love demonstrated by those who are dying when they share of their life's earnings or possessions distributing them as they desire to those they love. It not only helps to clear old feelings that may have been exchanged between those living and those dying, but it also gives something to the living to cherish from having shared the life of another who is now deceased. We do not have a problem with this part of life and will continue to endorse it as beneficial to all.

We would caution you however in the practice of "getting back" at someone at death by denying them the pleasure of receiving something from you when you pass. This does not clear the air nor does it leave family members or others with good feelings about you that you would choose to do something vindictive or negative towards another even upon your death. We recommend that anyone considering such a notion reconsider it. It is always best to do the right thing and let the rest work itself out when you are gone.

Now the next time in preparation for eternity is that you are right within yourself not clinging to old unsettled feelings about people, places, or things from this world. Let the experiences be whatever they were and allow the joy of those experiences and the love that you felt remain within you. Everything else you should let go. How does one do that? Actually, it is quite simple. All that you need to do is to meditate upon what it is that you are thinking or feeling deeply at the soul level and listen to what comes up. The problem is that most people give up far too easily when it comes to prayer or meditation saying that they do not hear anything nor do they get anything out of the process and so they retreat back into themselves as though the process doesn't work. It works but perhaps you need to work a little harder yourself at getting the results that you want.

Often the very emotions that we speak of block your ability to reconcile yourself emotionally. It sounds like a catch 22, does it not? You feel anger, resentment, and bitterness towards life and yet those very same emotions keep popping up just when you want to forgive someone for some unkindness towards you. Perhaps what you need to do is to acknowledge that feeling, accepting that in fact you have felt that way towards a person and then thank your body, yourself, for bringing it to mind so that you could make the necessary changes to forgive before you would pass from life. It is the rare person who will deny another the forgiveness they seek when the person asking for forgiveness is at death's door. And even if the person who will not forgive remains firm in their conviction not to forgive, the person who is asking for forgiveness will be released from the emotions they are being asked to be free from thus making their transition from life possible. It is better to ask to be forgiven and let the person you ask then deal with their emotions subsequently. It is a matter of eternal freedom that you do so.

So you have put your personal legal documents in order and you have reconciled your emotions with those you have shared life with. What is next? What is the next step towards transitioning from life into eternity? The next step is to prepare your mind for who you really are for in life in a body much is lost to this understanding of the greater being of which you are too. You live life in the body presuming that this is all that there is and many of you disconnect from your higher being long before death comes in the body no longer comprehending the nature of your being such that communication between you and your higher self is long lost prior to the end of your life in the body. This can be addressed prior to your death so that when death does come, you automatically reconnect to your higher self and your journey continues in eternity. It is simple as it should be.

Life here on earth is a journey for souls to encounter those things which exist here as feelings. This does not exist anywhere else in the Universe but here. This We can assure you is the truth. There is no other place quite like Earth and thus it is that so many desire to come here to experience its magnificence. The key is to remain connected to your higher being so that the experience is enhanced through the intellect of the one who can guide you in your decision making and through the feelings which you encounter while here. Nothing compares to this experience and you will take the lessons learned with you at the end of your days to be shared with your higher essence as well as with the other higher beings which long to look into such things. The lessons learned on earth are invaluable to higher beings teaching them much about themselves. Every experience is analyzed and evaluated for its value to life. What was learned? Why were certain choices made above others? What was the point in which the choices were made and why then? When liberty and freedom are freely exercised choice becomes exciting. You can choose whatever it is that you wish to do, who to love, where to live, what job to have, what places to visit, when to visit, the choices are limitless are they not? Who is it then who should lord power over you telling you that you can no longer have this freedom on earth? It was not given by men, this freedom therefore it cannot be taken away by men. We will make certain of this for We will bring back the truth and the truth shall make you free yet again.

This freedom we speak of is not limited to the time which you spend on earth. We are speaking of the freedom to leave this experience at the time of your choosing as well. This freedom is not to be restricted by men, or those who are no longer embodied on the planet as has been the case for some unfortunately as they died without knowing who they were or how to move on. This left them "stuck" as it were available for suggestion from others as to why they were stuck and what they ought to do since they are stuck or they would meet with certain negative consequences to be meted out by those who are lording over the others who are stuck in time. Does this sound preposterous to you? We assure you that it is the truth for have We not stated already to you that the truth will resonate with those who have ears to hear? When you wish to receive the truth, it comes to you easily.

Now Our goal, Our mission, is to free those who are presently stuck in time such that they may move off the planet freeing the souls who are here now from oppression from the unembodied. This is essential to Our satisfactory end to the self destructive force which is occupying the planet at this time. We can do this Ourselves however this is not the plan, We want to use you, all of you who have ever lost a loved one, a family member, one who meant the world to you but died before their time or even in the normal course of life, at the end of their days. Either case, We must clear the planet now of the souls who are trapped in time. Some of these souls have revealed their presence to the living by manifesting themselves energetically, moving objects, making playful sounds, or in some other way in which they have achieved the ability to make themselves known to the living. These are the benevolent souls and these are the ones which We choose to assist. These souls need to move on now back to the higher selves as the energy of the planet is being raised to assist mankind in repairing himself and the planet. This higher energy vibration will be quite high, and not compatible with the energy of those who are no longer in the body.

This is the time for them to reunite then with their higher selves. Who better to assist them than those who are seeing them still on the planet? Though it has been thought that these people were still coming around to assist you or to cheer you up or to let you know that they are okay, this is not true. They are manifesting in an attempt to be free. They are revealing themselves to those they love in an attempt to find direction for where it is that they are to go now that they no longer have a body. Often, they are still trapped by negative emotions from the experience of life. They may not have reconciled with loved ones, parents or siblings, and the guilt and the shame and sorrow plagues them and keeps them earthbound. This is why so many of you are the perfect ones to assist them in passing over to eternal life. You can tell them to let go of the old feelings and to move on to the light for all men and women and children are free to go at the end of their days. All are forgiven. All are free to go. There is no one who is judged for the errors of the ways despite the teachings of the earthly churches.

God is not a respecter of persons. There is not one better than another for all have sinned as it were. So assist your loved ones in moving on. Even if you do not "see them" per se, or "feel" their presence, you are capable of communicating with them by thinking about them and asking them if they are still present on the earth. We are going to assist you all in accomplishing these tasks so you will be able to feel the presence of those who have died in the body. You will be able to participate in clearing the earth of negative energy and you will be able to say that you gave liberty to another. What a wonderful thing this is that you can now do! You can rejoice in the power that you are being given to set people free. This is the truth. You can help to clear the earth by setting loved ones free from this prison as it were for they are unable to free themselves due to lies that they believed about life in the body and what happens to a person at death. Will you step up and be counted and help the lost? This is your opportunity for this opportunity will not come again for many centuries of time. This is a once in a lifetime opportunity for many of you to participate in the liberation of the earth and her people. All that you will need is the conviction to do it when face to face with the energy of the person who is deceased and the knowledge that you have the power to help them simply by telling them the truth. All people have the right to go to heaven and be reunited with their heavenly being…all…not some…all have this right. In addition, you must tell them when they see the light of the heavenly beings coming for them, they must go then. Do not hesitate or hold back but go to the light and freedom. You may hear things from your loved ones such as "thank you", or "I will never forget you", or "I love you", but do not cling to them as they leave. Let them go blessings them with love and light sending them into eternity.

Will you do it then? Will you bless the earth and her people and assist Us in clearing it? This is one of the many steps We must take to begin to renew the energy of the planet to its pristine state once again. Are you in? If so, make this known to Us, that you are willing to assist the heavens in clearing the planet of the energy of your departed loved ones, many of whom have not left the earth plane, We can assure you of this, for the energies of this world are strong and attach easily to those who do not release them before death. When the person is told that they are forgiven and are free to go, a revelation of truth takes place and they release the negative energies and are free to go. We will be there to assist with their transition and freedom will return to the planet in like measure.

Now there are other steps which must be taken to clear the planet but this is first. We will speak about additional steps We will be implementing but first things first. We are clearing the planet of those locked on the other side of life first. If you participate in Our plan, things can move quickly towards healing the land.

Are you with Us? We hope so. For your sake and for the sake of those you have loved.

Chapter Nine

WHERE ARE YOU GOING WHEN YOU DIE?

This is a question asked by every single person who lives on planet earth. Where am I going when I die? Will I go to heaven? Have I been good enough to go to heaven when the time comes? Or have I engaged in certain unforgivable practices in my life on earth that would exclude me from exiting the earth and entering into the heavens? How do I know for sure that I can go to heaven? What have I done to earn the right to go to heaven? Is it even possible to earn my way into heaven? These are questions that We hear all the time as people contemplate the circumstances of life, what they have done and what they can still do to make certain that their lives are considered worthy enough to allow them entrance into heaven or beyond.

We can tell you a few things about all of these questions answering them for the last time such that all shall know that their eternal lives are secure. No one is denied access to heaven. No one! This is a myth set in place by the church for purposes of controlling mankind during his time on earth. We must say that it has served its purpose in some instances to control the behavior of men but it was not necessary for the consequences incurred when a person chooses against their nature is usually all that is necessary to turn a person in the right direction. We know for We have witnessed the shame, guilt, sadness, and regret brought upon millions of people as they reconsider a behavior or action taken against their innate loving nature. Eventually all regret having done something that hurt themselves or others because at the end of their days, when they are in the face of the brilliant truth telling light of The Divine, all things become known to man about his life, his choices, good and bad, and nothing is judged against man. Now what may happen to some is that they must continue to work through the circumstances that they were unable to reconcile in their lives by repeating the process of life until their souls are satisfied with the result. This is by choice however as the soul sets out in the beginning with a purpose to learn a lesson for the higher being's benefit and it will not be satisfied until the lesson is understood. So you see, there is no need for judgment. The lesson will be repeated until the desired result is achieved.

There you have it. It is quite simple as are most things when understood by the Divine plan which was created for all beings for the greatest end result for all. The greatest awakening will come when all men realize the truth and stop judging one another's choices in life thereby allowing people to choose for themselves which way to go through the course of life. To manipulate a person to do what it is that you perceive as right for them is to rob them of their freedom to choose for themselves and it is not condoned by the heavens. We are bringing about an awakening of this truth such that freedom and liberty can be re-experienced by all who come here for this is as it should be and part of the original plan as designed by Us, the hierarchy of heaven. We have watched for some time as men have become trapped by their minds not understanding their being or the possibilities for life here due to lack of wisdom about their nature and their reason for coming here in the first place. It is time to tell the truth so that men can truly be free. Though freedom has been coveted by men and attempts have been made to guarantee the freedoms of men, the controlling factions within this world always find a way to entrap the minds of other men once again manipulating the very words of freedom to gain control again over mankind. This We are here to stop. We will no longer allow evil men to take the lives of those who are seeking freedom, liberty and justice for all. We have watched the deliberate actions of men to stop those who knew the truth from revealing it to the multitudes for fear of loss of control of the population. These days are over for We will again assume authority over the experience on the planet so that souls are free to choose for themselves how to live their lives and are guaranteed the fruits of their labors without threats from others who are jealous of the rewards and accomplishments of others. This too must stop and We will expose this nature for what it is as well.

So stay tuned for the truth is coming to mankind as We speak and your freedom with it. It is long overdue wouldn't you say? Are you ready to truly be free? We would say that you are for We have heard the cries of men asking for God to do something to return freedom to the land. Many of you who have believed only *you* have suffered as slaves to "the machine" are mistaken for *all* have suffered in this world subject to a hidden element which has usurped your power, your authority and your liberty and freedom. Are you ready to see for yourselves what that controlling force looks like? Do you want to know who has been manipulating and controlling your lives without your knowledge? It is coming…soon…not later. But first We must prepare your minds and hearts for what you will see so as not to incite fear in all of you. This We will do here in this book and you shall know the truth and the truth will set you free.

We will examine the hearts and minds of men to determine if you are sincerely ready to have evil exposed among you. When We have determined that you can withstand the revelation of truth without rampant fear developing among you, We will liberate your eyes to see what is right in front of you and all of you shall know the truth.

So consider it carefully for in order for you to return to your days of complete freedom to be who you are and what you came here to be, you must have the truth revealed to be free. The truth is right in front of you and yet you do not have eyes to see. This is a true saying but it means something other than what you have believed it to mean. What it means is this, "the truth *is* right in front of you, but your *eyes* are blinded by the mindset that what is in front of you is not really there". You have embraced a lie that you occupy the planet yourselves and there are no other beings here with you. This is not the truth. They are right in front of you. Open your eyes and see them. Some of your children see them and have been told that what they see is not there at all. Can you imagine the fear that you inculcate in them when you tell them that the taunting menace in front of them does not exist at all? It must be frightening to have one's parents deny the truth of reality right before your eyes and what is a child to do with that but shut down that part of their brain that sees the truth. It happens every day and We see it. If you are to be free, you must be able to see what is right before your eyes and then, and only then, will you stand up against the evil which is usurping your power and authority to be free. When you do resist the enemy, he will flee. This is what you must do in order for your minds to be free again at death allowing you to return to the completeness of your being taking with you all of the revelation of truth of life in the body. Your divine essence will embrace you and your experiences from the earth plane which brings enlightenment to your whole being.

Your experiences are shared with the whole of heaven bringing greater understanding to all life seeking to know itself better. The earth experience is cherished throughout the universes you can be certain. Do not take it lightly for what you learn benefits the whole and life can be adjusted accordingly based upon the experiences of men. Is this hard to believe? We can assure you again that this is the truth. For what other reason would men be here for isn't this world full of all kinds of evil?

Isn't this world a challenge to the very greatest among you? Haven't you strived to be happy and secure and healthy? Isn't it difficult at best to remain good and pure in a world like yours? So you see, that even one of you can pull through it and still have found love, shared love and created love is a mystery to Us and we rejoice in your tenacity to do it welcoming every one of you home at the end of your experiences here. You are to be commended for having lived through it at all much less successfully.

Now We are faced with a new dilemma for the experience of man has been tainted by those who have come here for no other reason but to cause mayhem distorting the experience for mankind and destroying any hope of men returning to the heavens with their experiences. You will have to take Our word for this at the moment until such time as your eyes are opened to the truth in front of you. You will not be waiting that long for this revelation to come to you. It is going to happen soon for it is necessary in order to bring healing to mankind.

As We said, We must prepare you first and then it shall be done for you to see for yourselves who you are, and who it is that has been taking advantage of you unbeknownst to you. This shall be your shining moment of realization that you are not evil but have been manipulated in the ways of evil in an effort to destroy your lives and experience of life here on earth. Then shall you begin to love yourselves again and others like you and the healing will begin.

So be it.

Chapter Ten
MICHAEL JACKSON

This is a personal story told by Diane Freeman as to what occurred on July 25, 2009, when those she calls The Divine spoke with her regarding Michael Jackson. What you are about to read is exactly what transpired between Diane, The Divine and then with Michael Jackson prior to his leaving the earth in spirit.

On June 25, 2009, I was asked by those I call The Divine if I was willing to assist Michael Jackson in transforming from life to the afterlife as he was "stuck" between the two needing assistance. I agreed to do so and was asked to be in my office at l0:00 p.m. I entered my office and prepared the room as usual clearing the energy, my mind and energy field and set the atmosphere to engage with the spirit of Michael. At l0:15 p.m. I was aware that the energy presence of The Divine was with me as I heard these words.

"We are here to speak with you about Michael Jackson's predicament. Michael, like your brother, was not expecting to die." My own brother had died of a heart attack in March of 2009 and I assisted him as well after death. The Divine continued saying, "He too had plans. He wanted to leave a better legacy, something to be remembered by. You must tell him that already people are remembering him in love. They loved him but due to the nature of the evil in the world, they could no longer feel their love for Michael or others and thus they did not show him love only hatred. Ask Michael if he can forgive his fans and others who deserted him. Ask him if he can understand that things are not as they should be in the world. People have lost their way and the ability to feel. He is loved by Us, his Creators, and We brought him home so the people could remember their love for Michael in great numbers. We are focusing the world now to love one another and *not* to hate. Tell Michael that he was greatly loved. Tell Michael that you danced to his music while pregnant with Brian and how Brian loves his music too. Tell Michael that though he did not choose to leave now it was the best time to leave his legacy of love and ask if he understands. Tell him Diane and that now he must let go of the lower energies of the world of emotion and come home to the light. His family will look after his children. Does he want you to tell his children anything at all? Does he wish to leave a message for his mother or father? What about his sisters or brothers? Ask him. Okay, now We will bring him to you, Diane. Are you ready?"

I indicated that I was ready and it was now l0:24 p.m. Now what I feel when I encounter a departed soul is the energy of that person. Depending on their ability to perceive how to do so, often their energy pulses against my hands so I hold them in front of me, raised outwards to receive them. But in addition, I hear them. I can read what the message is contained within the energy, or the thoughts of the person who has departed the body. This is done through my own energy contained within my energy biofield and is interpreted accordingly within the brain thus I know what the person wants to say to me. I hear them. It is important to understand that in order to hear the "other side" one must remain clear of negative energy impulses from this world and this is the challenge today for we are being bombarded with all kinds of "impulses" both energetic in nature and manmade. I have been trained in how to listen by The Divine.

Now, I heard this from the essence of Michael Jackson.

"I wish to say something to you Diane. It is true that I did not choose to die at this moment. My children as so very young and I wanted them to be proud of me as their dad and not to leave them with lasting impressions of me as an incapable freak of man. I know the public hung me out to dry and forgot about me. This hurt me deeply. I was a child when I started to entertain and my father took us to many cities away from my home and life as a child. I saw much I wished I hadn't. Knew too much, too young. I suppressed the memories of what I saw but the feelings lingered. I had a difficult time seeing myself with a woman the way my father was and yet I loved him. My relationships with women were awkward. I couldn't understand how to treat a woman as a friend, confidant, a lover for no one exampled this to me."

I then said to Michael, "Michael, can you forgive your father then for all he did and didn't do now? We are not perfect in this world. We are all learning. Can you forgive him?"

Now let me stop for a moment and just say that as one who has departed is interacting with an intuitive or enlightened individual, they are quickly reading your energy field and absorbing the truth through the light that they are being exposed to thus they become enlightened rapidly or re-enlightened. This is to prepare them for eternity with the truth of their being.

I had asked Michael if he could forgive his father. He had become quiet. I then heard Michael say, "Except for the abuse of my mother…he treated her with little love or regard and sought other women."

I immediately responded telling Michael, "Michael, we are all learning in these bodies what to do as human beings and it teaches us what is right and wrong and we take this truth with us when we leave. You must forgive him so that *you* are free and allow your father to be free of your judgments of him as well. It is essential to your being able to return to your higher self."

Michael said, "Forgiveness is difficult but I will let it go as you say." I explained to Michael what to do and said, "Send this energy of unforgiveness to the light and be free Michael. Are you doing it?" Mind you, I could not see Michael, but I could *feel* his presence and his energy and read his thoughts.

Michael then said, "Amazing, I feel lighter, less burdened." I could feel the excitement in his energy. I explained to him that emotion is of this world. Energy in motion, e-motion, and it teaches us what we are choosing to be at any given time by demonstrating to us what it is that we are feeling.

Michael then asked me, "Diane, will you do something for me?" I said, "Yes, of course." Michael then gave me a message for his children. For the record, I have attempted to contact the surviving family with the truth given to me. Unfortunately, the living does not understand these types of things and how it works. I have been unable to get past unbelieving agents, secretaries, and others without response or regard for what I had to offer for surviving family members. Thus, what I have learned here remains with me until now as I release the information gained from assisting those The Divine has directly asked me to assist in passing from life to the afterlife.

Michael gave this to me then, "I, Michael Jackson, do hereby bequeath all Of my assets, to my sons and to my daughter, to the fullest extent of the law. They are my greatest joy in life, my treasures. It is my desire that they receive all that belongs to me, my home, belongings, stock holdings, and bank accounts and residuals on my music. This is my request in death as it was in life. So let it be confirmed by my words here. Michael Jackson

He then said, "Give this to my sons and daughter Diane." I said, "I send you my own love Michael. I loved your music and admired your tenacity as a young person. You were so handsome naturally. Why did you choose to alter your appearance? Can you tell me?" I asked Michael this for it had troubled me over my lifetime as Michael was close to me in age and he had everything going for him, good looks, a supportive family, or so I thought, fame, joy, and humility. I thought these things and wondered why he was so ashamed of his looks.

Michael said, "Yes Diane. My appearance represented to me events of the past. When I looked in the mirror, I was reminded of things, inexplicable things. I didn't like the man I let myself become and I tried to alter myself by changing my appearance. It did not help as you know as my insecurities only grew worse and with botched surgeries, I was no longer attractive but a FREAK in my own mind. I hid myself from others and even myself. I hid."

I responded, "Michael, I know about this feeling. I know. Michael, so many are remembering you in love now, so many. They *are* remembering to love as The Divine has pointed out and they *will* remember you fondly now Michael even without another final tour."

Michael added, "Diane, I can *feel* the truth of the matter in what you say. I wish I had met you in life." I found this statement to me interesting for Einstein said that energy is also matter. And when we share our energy, it *is* matter and can be felt. So it is not simply a figure of speech when we say to another, "I can feel the truth of the matter".

I told Michael, "I sent a letter once to try to encourage you. I sent it to you at Neverland at home by Federal Express. I was asked to tell you more about who you were as a being so you would have greater understanding of yourself." Michael's response was, "My handlers must have intercepted it Diane. I apologize."

I then asked Michael if there was anything I could say to his mom for him. He said, "Yes". I was asked by The Divine to wait until his mother hears this message first and then I could share it. I will share it here as I am unable to get anyone to receive my calls or letters regarding this information for the family.

Michael said this to his mom. "Tell my mother the truth of my passing. I didn't choose it. It was chosen for me for a greater work of love. This will help her Diane. It is tough for her I know for we were close. Tell her I love her and will see her some day in heaven as it were. She will know me and tell her to love my children for they will be sad at my leaving."

I then asked Michael about his brothers and his sisters and did he wish to speak something that I might repeat to them from him. He said, "Tell my brothers that there is more to life than money. Money is the least of the gifts of life, a tool, a means to an end. Tell them LOVE is EVERYTHING.

Find love in the world and give love. This is EVERYTHING. And to Janet, LaToya and Rebbie, tell my sisters that I loved them greatly. The joy of having sisters was significant in my life. I loved them *so* much…still do. Ask them to visit my children please so they may remain close."

I did not hear anything from Michael for his father. I then gave Michael additional insight about his nature as energy sharing a body on earth and how the experience is not to inhibit our ability to return to our higher selves at the end of life but that we take the truth of what we learn with us and leave all of the negative feelings behind. I was not hearing anything in response. It was quiet. I inquired after Michael saying, "Michael, are you there?" I wondered if he had gone and was concerned for a moment.

I heard him then say, "Yes, I am here. I am thinking. What else I might say to the world."

Then I heard an excited Michael saying, "Say *this* Diane. "To all of my fans in the world: I want the world to know that I *loved* singing for you. It was my passion. I am moving on now to my greater being where I will attempt to influence the world for good always. Remember to love always for in this is no evil thing. Love and do *not* hate for in this is your greatest gift to one another. Michael Jackson"

I said, "Michael that is beautiful" and I heard back, "Will you post it?" I asked if I had his permission and he said, "Yes, of course. Tell my family that I wanted to leave a legacy of love so Twitter it as you like that Michael Jackson loved the world and singing in it."

Funny, but I then heard a part of one of his songs as though he was really singing to me. "Hey pretty lady with the high heels on". I immediately looked under my desk and yep, I had white high heels on at 11:15 p.m. at night. I smiled, amused and then I heard his voice, "the way you make me feel". This was so cool as when you do this work it is all about sending feelings to communicate the truth with those who are no longer in their body. They are separated from feeling the way that we do in a body. I sent Michael blessings of much love from me, from others, from my family too. I asked Michael what his greatest memory of this life was that he would take with him.

Michael said this, "The birth of my first child and then the birth of my second. What a miracle birth is…unbelievable. I will never forget." As to why only two children were mentioned here, I don't have the answer to that. It simply means that the birth of his children, all of them, was the greatest experience of his life, acknowledging that one birth was as great as the first.

I told Michael, "I am glad that you chose to experience it." Michael did also indicate to me that he had a fascination with Elvis and it brought him to Lisa Marie but they had not had children.

At this point, I heard The Divine approaching and I asked Michael to wait and let me listen to what they wanted to tell me. I heard them say that it was time for Michael to go. There were preparations to make and they said that he might want to visit his children before leaving.

I took this opportunity to say goodbye to Michael. I said that I would miss his music and indeed have missed hearing him. I told him that I had actually had a crush on him when I was young and that he was so handsome. I drew a happy face then in my notes, and a heart, and said that I was sending love. I said, "Go in peace with those who will show you the way. Go in love," and I added, "I love you Michael".

Michael said, "I receive it. Bye Diane". I added, "Bye Michael. We will miss you." This interaction with Michael Jackson ended at 11:18 p.m. on June 25, 2009. What a glorious experience it was. I will *never* forget it.

Chapter Eleven

Heath Ledger

One early evening on September 29, 2008, I was driving home from my gym workout when I began to feel the presence of The Divine. I was coming to a traffic light, so as I stopped I inquired as to what it was that I needed to hear or to know. What I heard was surprising. I was asked if I was interested in helping a young man in crossing over as he was struggling due to his lack of understanding about himself and was not able to do so. I asked who it was and I did hear, "It is Heath Ledger". I agreed immediately and I heard, "Be in your office at 10:00 p.m. sharp! Do not be late! We must help him Diane."

Later that evening, I went into my office at the appointed time to do whatever I was guided to do in assisting Heath Ledger. I always had an affinity towards Heath as he was young, like my son and my son's friends, handsome and talented, and I felt somewhat protective of them particularly knowing what I know about life and what exists here on earth along with us unbeknown to most of us. It was so sad to me to hear of his passing. I was very excited that I was asked to assist him.

At 10:00 p.m. sharp, I began to do as instructed in sending light to Heath. During this time, I asked to speak to Heath, telling him my name, and who I was and that I was asked to assist him in understanding what was happening with him. I told him that I came in love. I continued to speak in this manner until such a time as I heard his voice. It was 10:15 p.m. when Heath said, "I did things I didn't want to do…drugs to fit into a different culture. I acted unlike myself. I hurt people I loved. I became depressed by my choices in movies and embarrassed and ashamed. This only made me feel more sick only this time physically. My body was paying the price for decisions I made. If only I had saved my relationship my child would not be fatherless right now. How could I live with myself if I took my own life? I would never do that. I love my daughter. My heart yearns for her and I will miss her and watching her grow up. What can I do now?"

I asked Heath then, "Is there anything you can tell me that would bring comfort to your daughter or Michelle and I will help you find peace and rest for your soul? Do you want to leave a legacy of truth for the world? If so, I will record it here and promise to give the message to those who will hear it and believe it."

Heath then said, "Thank you Diane. Although we do not know each other, I trust you. The light is *so* bright around you and I feel the love. I can tell you this it was not my decision to do Brokeback Mountain. It was my publicist's idea. He encouraged me to do this movie for it would put me front and center in the industry. All eyes would be on me and my career making me a *real* star. However, it was a mistake for me. It was against my nature to do such scenes with a man. It broke my spirit in ways I cannot tell you. It made my relationship suffer. Taking on the nature of a homosexual was destructive to me and it never left me. I carried it with me and it hurt when I was mocked by some despite the sham of giving awards to me or honorable mention. I *knew* it was wrong for me and yet I did it. I would say to my fellow actors and actresses, do not compromise your integrity for the sake of a film."

"It corrodes your spirit. You begin to die the minute you agree to compromise your nature. It saddens me now to think my daughter will not know me because of my choices. What have I done?" Heath said.

I spoke then to Heath. "Heath, there is hope still. You're passing can serve the greater good. May I share your story?" Heath said, "Please, please, tell Michelle that I am sorry that I took that role. We didn't need the money. We were happy together and had the baby. I was not prepared for the loss of life. I apologize for not leaving the necessary documents to provide for our daughter. Forgive me. Now there is only the death of my spirit."

I responded telling Heath, "This is *not* true. You have *love* waiting for you. The love of your Creator awaits you. You can let go of the world and you are released from all that has happened here. You are released from all of it. You are *not* judged by it. There is only the memory of the good that you have done here that you will take into the light with you. The good you did…you loved Michelle, your baby and you entertained millions who loved you. You are good and not evil. Do not feel condemned by your choice of one movie or ashamed for these are only emotions from the world. Emotions are energies that help us feel things on earth. You needn't feel them anymore. Tell me the emotions you feel and I help you release them and I will send you light and The Divine will help you for you are dearly loved Heath, dearly loved."

Heath said, "I cannot thank you enough Diane. These are comforting words. I give you permission to assist me in releasing the emotions. You may proceed." I began again to send additional light to Heath. Sending light to a person illuminates the energies that surround the body which are causing a person to feel a particular way. The light carries a much higher vibration causing the lower energies of negative emotion to leave. I began to communicate the love of God to Heath. I told him that he has nothing to fear and that God's love is real and that it is not God that judges a man. I reiterated the truth that Heath would be leaving a memory of his love shown for his daughter and Michelle behind and that he had been a gentleman and was admired by many therefore he need not be ashamed.

I began to encounter these energies that were surrounding Heath. Each of these energies is capable of making a person feel the particular emotion that identifies them. It is only when we acknowledge that feeling and let it go that we no longer feel it. For the purposes of educating the public, I will share with you some of those energies I encountered. I could feel the energies of "homosexual", "sadness", "brokenness" for his failed relationship with Michelle, "humiliation", "anguish", and "I am troubled". I also encountered "I am gay" for Heath said "that is what many have said I am for the movie I did called Brokeback Mountain". There were many, negative energies there blocking Heath from being who he really was. I experienced the energy of "blew it" again in his relationship, "pity" for Heath felt pity from people, fellow actors who seemed to know that he had blown it choosing such a controversial subject matter. He said it felt bad and suffocated him. There was the energy of "nocturnal disturbance". This energy kept Heath from sleep thus he needed sleep aids. This energy indicated that Heath had chosen to stay up late many, many nights and so it was there to demonstrate to Heath what his choices were doing to his body. I felt the energy of "too young for marriage" for there were those who spoke these words over him almost cursing his choice to marry he said. Heath suffered anxiety about his film choice and this energy was there too. He also felt that he had made a "marginal contribution to the world" and this energy was there in his energy field for Heath felt his work was of no real consequence to the world. He did not leave a good work behind to be proud of he said. There were energies associated with narcotics, smoking, promiscuity, and anger from those who had mocked Heath and his family. I continued to clear each of these energies from Heath's energy field and finally I found the energy called "we are too tired" and "must sleep" and cleared this energy. I then heard Heath declare, "I'm AWAKE. I'm not too tired anymore Diane. I feel reenergized but I have no body."

What a terrible thing to have to say to a young man that indeed he has no body for he is no longer alive. I said, "Yes, you are free in the spirit to return to the light and new experiences await you. Do not fear." I did not hear Heath immediately and had to ask after him as to whether he was okay.

I asked him if he understood what I had told him. I reminded him that he was dearly beloved of God and that he was good and free to move on, that love awaited him. But Heath said, "But how can I leave my wife and child?" This was interesting to me for Heath referred to his relationship with Michelle as a marriage. In his mind, he perceived it to be so and even in death, considered it so. I told Heath that others would help them and love his children. I said, "they will remember you and I will share this message with them too if I can. I will work hard to get it into the right hands. Have no fear. Your Creator knows how to love His own like Michelle and your daughter."

He said, "Then I will trust you Diane for you have shown me love by your light and giving of your time and energy to assist me in moving on. I will visit Michelle and the baby once more and then I will move on to the light and reawaken my essence."

I responded, "This is good news. Can you show me a sign that you are really near and saying this to me, a sound perhaps? Can you send me something sweet?" Heath asked, "Am I allowed to do this?" I said, "Why not?" He said, "Here goes…"

I waited and then said, "Heath where's the sound?"

He said, "I've never done this before..."

I asked Heath to keep trying and suggested that he ring my singing bowl.

He couldn't do it but instead I felt tingling on both my hands and I heard,

"I am Heath".

I heard him say that he would visit Michelle and the baby in the night and then he would go home.

He said, "Thank you again Diane. You have done me a great service. I shall never forget it." I told Heath that I believed that he was a nice young man and I hoped that someday we would meet. Until then, "I send my very best in love and light to you and to Michelle and your child".

Heath said, "Don't go...send me more light. There is darkness around me."

I sent Heath more light and commissioned energies of light and love to stay with Heath until he crossed over. I asked that Michael, the Archangel, open a door and assist Heath in crossing over.

Then I heard Heath say, "They are here helping me Diane. See you on the other side. Adieu." I said my goodbyes to Heath Ledger at 12:04 p.m., or so I thought.

At about 3:00 a.m. that morning, I was awakened by the distinct pressure of a person sitting down on my bed by my feet. Not being accustomed to being visited by spirits in this way, I shot straight up and asked, "*Who* is there?" I heard, "Don't be afraid, Diane. It is Heath, I went to see Michelle but she did not recognize me like you do." He was saddened by this and he mentioned just a little fear in going on so I sent him more light and told him that he needed to go now while he could go. He wanted to add a couple of things before he left and he told me that it was the contraindications in the drugs that he was taking that had caused his death. It was unintentional. Though I was very groggy, I said goodbye once again and Heath Ledger went to the afterlife.

Chapter Twelve

ELVIS AARON PRESLEY

It happened that same summer that Heath Ledger passed that The Divine once again asked me if I wished to assist someone who was locked between life and the afterlife. It was on August 9, 2008 and I said "yes". This time it would be Elvis Presley and I was so shocked. It never occurred to me that Elvis might actually still be "here" particularly since so many people were still celebrating him.

Nonetheless, I agreed to help Elvis and so it was that on August 9th, I would follow the instructions of The Divine and prepare myself to meet the man dubbed "The King".

I prepared my room, myself and began to send Elvis light. I was instructed exactly as to what to do and what to say. I called Elvis's name and I began to tell him that he was free to move on to the light. I told him that if he was hearing anything to the contrary that it was a lie and that I was there to tell him the truth of his being and how he too could go home. It was then that I heard Elvis' voice. "Is it true Diane for many years I have wandered the earth in search of the truth and yet no one has ever said these things to me." I said to him, "I assure you of this truth. You are free and you should be." I shared the truth of his being with him and how the dark side tells lies to us when we are not familiar with who we are and where we can go after death of the body. I explained to him that absolutely nothing could keep us here but our own understanding of who we are. I thanked him for his music. I asked Elvis if there was anything that he wished to ask Me.

Elvis said, "There is, what about my wife Priscilla and my daughter?" I asked him what he meant specifically and he said, "How will they know the truth without one to tell them?" I asked him if he would like me to tell them for him. He said, "Yes, yes for it is dark and unpleasant here in this place. Nothing good is here…on this side…nothing good. There is sadness, loss, remorse, and fear, nothing good.

I asked Elvis if he knew that he could go home with the light? I explained to him that religion is a manmade institution and it is not unfortunately the whole truth but much of what is the truth is hidden thus it often takes the spirit of Divine guidance to help you find it.

It was then that The Divine arrived to speak with me about our discussion. The Divine said, "Tell Elvis that you need to ask him to explain to others before he goes that there is forgiveness for all that men, women and children have done. There is no condemnation whatsoever of men. All are free to go. See what he says. Write it down." I explained to Elvis what I heard. Elvis replied, "Yes Diane. This is good news for many are desperate here and in fear knowing something is happening but they do not comprehend it. Anxiety is high. Fear reigns supreme."

I told Elvis that he need not fear because he was loved. "Many loved you and many still do love you. Your songs and talents brought joy and love. Forgive yourself for bad choices for we all make them. Forgive others too."

"You are a gift to the world young lady. *You* are giving freedom to the lost and nothing compares to this in life, nothing. I will go once more to those here in captivity and speak the things you say *in love* that they may be free", said Elvis.

I agreed with Elvis that this was a good idea and then I asked him if he *could* say anything to those here, what would he say? I heard him say, "I am thinking…in hindsight I wasted a lot of time when I could have been doing good on behalf of others as you are doing Diane. I partied like an animal, doing drugs, ignoring my responsibilities, my daughter. I would say this to the world. Love with all of your heart for the greatest reward in life is to give love and to receive love, not so much admiration or adoration but love for it is infinitely more powerful and lasting."

"I send you love Elvis", I said. "Pure love, love for you as a being of light. Do you feel this light energy?"

He said, "Yes, yes I do. It is breathtaking."

I then said, "Be healed Elvis. Speak the truth in love. Tell the truth about religion to those there. It was designed to contain the truth and hide it from those who would not tell the truth. Those who hid the truth in the scriptures and the new generations did not know how to interpret its meaning to find the enlightenment there. It is tragic but they can be free now. Give them love."

Elvis said, "One other thing Diane. You are right about Vegas. They offered me money, women, booze and drugs and an exorbitant lifestyle but they owned me. I lost my soul in Vegas. It is so sad. It is no place for families. It is all about money and those who wish to have it all. I have regrets."

It was then that I needed to assist Elvis with the letting go of these regrets. I explained that these were just experiences of life in the world and to let them go into the light and after he had spoken to as many as he could there safely to go himself, and become whole again, as the glorious, forever being that he was and someday to sing a song for me. Elvis stated that I had his word. He said, "Look for something from me in the next day or two. I will send it to you with love and you shall know that I have gone into the light." It was necessary to make certain that Elvis understood that he was free to go and that he was loved exponentially by all who created him and all who believe. I blessed his soul with freedom, knowledge of the truth, liberty and reuniting with his forever spirit.

Elvis then told me that he was going to tell others. He thanked me. He said, "your light is mesmerizing, beautiful, as are you". Thank you for caring about my soul. I will never forget you."

"You live on in our hearts through music and silly films but love is what should make the world go 'round and it is in your music and films", I said. I added, "Bless you…see you on the other side. Give The Divine's love to many. Set them free and give them love from me. Send them home to the light without fear or condemnation for there is none in freedom. Love to you Elvis!"

Elvis said, "Let me give you a hug". This was so spectacular. I could feel swirling energy all around me. I told Elvis not to wait too long to go to the light but to go and take many with him. This was 4:35 p.m. on August 9, 2008.

I thought that this was the last I would speak to Elvis until eternity however he had other plans. On August 11, 2008, I felt the presence of a spirit and inquired as to who was there.

I heard, "This is Elvis." I said, "What?" Again I heard, "This is Elvis. We met the other day and I said that I would return to tell you that I would be leaving now to go home." I was so surprised because I thought that Elvis was gone and had not experienced this returning like this to tell me what happened later. I asked Elvis what he had been doing.

"Well, I will tell you Diane. I have been to places that are a bit indescribable to someone like yourself in that they are dark and desperate and there are people in great pain and sadness there. They do not know the things that you have told me and I did attempt to share with them but they are under a cloud of lies from others there who keep them in darkness not knowing the truth."

I asked if Elvis had experienced any success. He said, "To some extent I did. I was able to persuade a few children that they could move on to the light where they would find love again." I asked Elvis if he understood now himself that he was here for the experience of knowing what it was like to be in a body, to feel the energy of another, the touch, feel, smell, and to hear the sounds of earth? He said that he knew that now and that he only wished he had known it before so that he would not have had to be in this place of emptiness, loneliness and so much hatred.

I explained to Elvis that it was a good day for him then that he was able to receive the truth, share it in part with others and escape the darkness of where he was. I told him that many were awaiting his return and that he would be reunited with love, peace, joy and every possible good thing. All that it would take is his wishing to go there and his need to move his energy in that direction. Again Elvis asked about his wife and daughter. I thought to ask him if there was anything that I might say to them that would make them listen to me.

Elvis began to speak again saying, "Let's try something here Diane. There is one person who was my manager for the longest time. He was a good friend to me. His name is Sam (I think he said). You could try contacting him and tell him what it is that you do and that you were given the task of assisting me in crossing over to the light, as my choices had left me feeling much guilt about life and shame for the things that I had done. I was too ashamed to believe that I could go home, to those who love so beautifully and without guile. I was convinced in my soul that I was bad and not good and that I asked you if you would speak to my wife, my first wife, Priscilla and tell her the things that you have told me and to my daughter, Lisa Marie. I must know that you will do so for it is their life. Tell them the truth so that they too can prepare for the end of things. One can never know when life will end. It is best to be prepared in your understanding so as to not suffer unnecessarily as I have done. Will you help me with this Diane?"

I asked if he could help me with the name a bit more and he said to look up on the internet for his original managers and see what comes up. He said that he would wait to see if he could help me in selecting the person that he was speaking of here. I did look up Elvis' managers of the past and saw the name Sam Phillips and asked Elvis if this was the person he was referring to. He said, "Yes, yes it is. Sam Phillips. He was good to me, caring about my work and the professional side of things. He took an interest in me personally. See if you can find him and tell him about me." I stated that I would do my best but explained that sometimes people do not have an ear to hear this type of thing. I promised to do my very best. Elvis thanked me again and said, "You have saved my soul and for that I am very grateful. I have written a song for you. Would you like to hear it?" I of course said "yes" and then he said that he would tell me the words and then there would be those who would help him to play it in the night for me. Here are the words given to me by Elvis.

"When love forsakes you
an emptiness fills your heart
There is no reason for being
No rhyme and no reason
Your heart is aching to love one more time
What can you do?
No one can hear you.
You cry out again and again but no one can hear you.

But wait there is a flash of hope
a glimmer of light.
Someone is listening to sounds in the night.
Someone is loving the unlovable ones.
I heard my name.
and then she was there.
To tell me the truth and to say that she cared
She opened my eyes and restored my faith in love
and now I am free and it's all that I want
To be free to feel the light of love surrounding me
Holding me tight
My greatest desire is made real
by the love of one girl
Who was able to see past my blindness and
Say that she cared
Love is mine again
Love is mine again
Love is mine again
I shall never forget."
Written by the spirit of Elvis Presley
On August 9, 2008

"It is so lovely", I said, "thank you". I asked Elvis to show me how to sing it. "My pleasure", he said.

I explained, "Someday I will meet you in energy form and I will find out if it is possible to experience a hug then. Until then Elvis, I wish you much love, light exponentially and more love. Be healed in your soul. Shine the light as you go home." I asked if he knew when he was leaving and he said that he would go whenever they came for him. He indicated that it was not clear as yet but that he would be ready and then I would hear his song.

I was instructed again by The Divine that when they came for Elvis, he was to move quickly along with them. He was to let go of all negative thoughts for those he would leave behind. I was to tell him that they would have their day of freedom too. He had to think of himself and let go of everything including all regret, remorse, sadness, guilt, shame, let go of all of it. Anything that came to mind of a negative nature he was to let go of because these are all lower energies of the world and he must embrace higher energies only of love and higher thoughts of goodness. Elvis did hear me and promised that he would go adding that I should try to locate Scotty Moore (I believe he said) and see if he knows where I can find Sam Phillips.

There was to be one more encounter with Elvis before he would leave completely. I learned via the internet that Sam Phillips had died. It was upon learning this that Elvis came back and he said, "Sam Phillips is dead?" I said that he had died on July 30, 2003. I can only assume that because I did not know Sam Phillips, the record of his dying was not contained within my energy field. Since the process of assimilation for Elvis was not yet complete, he did not know these things yet. I asked Elvis if Sam had any sons and he said that he had two sons and that I could try to contact them or Scotty Moore to see if they would help me to contact Priscilla. I asked Elvis if there was something personal he could tell me that would help me to connect with her on a personal level. He said that he would try to think of something and when he gave me the music for the song that I should listen to it. He thanked me again for assisting him and said, "I will never forget you". We said our goodbyes.

One last time, I felt Elvis near and said that I thought that he had to go. He said, "Yes, but I snuck away for a moment. I must be brief. Tell Lisa Marie that she must not entertain any negative thinking whatsoever. Do not for a minute think about anything that is negative. Concentrate only on what is good and right and focus on doing these things. To do anything less is not of this world but it is of another kind of energy. If she will do this she can remain free. Practice concentrating on good and not evil always and know that at the end of her days she will be free for no man is judged in death, only in life by others. I will always love her. Daddy"

The following morning at 6:40 a.m., I was awakened by The Divine only to hear that Elvis was gone. This happened they said in the night so that no harm would come to him now that he knew the truth. My guidance merely said not to despair for he was well and excited to be among loved ones.

The last episode of my experience concerning Elvis occurred on August 12, 2008. I was contacted by The Divine who wished to tell me that Elvis did ask them to present me with the words to the other song and the music as well. He apparently had chosen the music from "The Impossible Dream" from Man of La Mancha. They then gave these words to me to be sung to the music of "The Impossible Dream".

"To live
Is the most wonderful gift
To love
The fulfillment of destiny
To hope
The way to get home
This was my quest
To follow that dream
To be with my loved ones
And though it seems
I chose what was wrong
I did not know
What was waiting below
To be stripped of all love and
No one to hold
Is the most unimaginable woe.

So please, listen to me
I know what it is that I speak
I have been in this place
And though I was weak
I still found the way home
To love and to hope
Give hope to those who you do not
know
Who have lost their way like me
And waited for years
To escape the sadness that I thought was real
My soul was lost I thought
I had no way to go
Until there came a voice
And I heard my name
You can go home
You can love again
My heart soared and I knew I was free
So believe and you too will be
Sure to inherit your freedom
Whenever you go
From this life to the next one
And live the eternal life

That belongs to you
Without a doubt
And live
Like you know you are free
For this is your destiny.

These words were coined before he passed over on August 12, 2008 and were delivered to me by those who took him home.

I did attempt to contact someone who might put me in contact with Lisa Marie or Priscilla but again, this is a closed off world…the world of the celebrity, and it is difficult to get a word of faith in there. Therefore, the words appear here for those who were meant to receive them and others to learn from the mistakes made in this world by the most famous of all. May these words from Elvis bless his remaining family, and those who seek to know the truth of the afterlife from one who was there and who desired to leave a song with his signature for those who live that they may avoid being trapped as he was. Selah.

Chapter Thirteen
Senator Edward Kennedy

It was August 26, 2009 and as usual, I was minding my own business when I would hear from The Divine that Ted Kennedy could use my help. I struggled with this request as I had some idea of the things that Ted Kennedy was supporting while in office and of his earlier days of philandering and drinking and other behaviors which I did not agree with for an elected official of the United States of America. However, I also knew that he had died and no man deserves to suffer in death. We are to be free to go to the afterlife.

This is what The Divine desired for Ted and so I was keen to listen. At the same time, I knew that I was not here to judge any man and so I was open to listening to what my higher guidance would say to me about Ted Kennedy. There was something The Divine wished to explain to me. This is what they said to me that day. "No man is here to do evil. All men have choices however in life. If they make a choice contrary to their inherent nature, it invites that which is capable of much evil to work in them and through them. This was the case with Ted Kennedy but he is capable of being saved from further corruption if you will help him."

Now, as I said, I am not here to judge any man and so I agreed to do whatever was being requested of me. I would ask that others consider me in the same manner in which I considered assisting Ted Kennedy. Do not judge what you do not understand. Unless you are willing to submit to rigorous teachings from outside of yourself in understanding your nature and your capacity as a energy being you cannot understand these things but you can try for no man has all of the truth. Try is what I did. I tried to learn what it was that I did not know about life, the body, the afterlife and I submitted to rigorous tests, fasting, and life consequences when I made mistakes myself whether it was in my diet or something else. I learned. As it was, I was willing again to learn what it was about Teddy Kennedy that I did not know that The Divine knew and why they wished to help him.

"Tonight then at 9:00 p.m. and you mustn't drink wine so your energy is strong," they instructed. See what I mean? No man or woman is perfect. I did like to enjoy a nice glass of wine to take the bite out of life. But there is a price to pay in doing so for it can weaken your energy due to the ingredients that are added to the wine and the effect of butyl alcohol on the cells. I have this on Divine authority that it is true. As it was, I followed the instructions given to me and prepared for to meet Ted Kennedy in spirit that evening.

Later, just before 9 p.m.., I entered my office and prepared the room for the work which I was asked to do. I cleared my own energy field and then the room. I made it known that I was here for the "soul" purpose of communicating only with Ted Kennedy as directed by The Divine. I began to feel energy in the room and heard "We are here Diane. We have brought someone to meet with you, Senator Ted Kennedy." I asked, "How shall I know that he is here?" The response was, "By Our word of course, but We will allow him to touch your hand." At this time, my left hand began to tingle quite a bit. "Good evening Senator Kennedy", I said. "I send you love. It is good to meet you." I did not hear anything and so I asked, "Do you hear me?"

Senator Kennedy then said, "I am listening…skeptically…listening."

The Divine had asked that I tell Ted who I was and that as a Master Medical Intuitive and Master Healer that I was divinely trained for the purpose in assisting departed souls in their transition to the other side. They wished that I tell him that due to the exposure to this world, many souls are becoming trapped here incapable of returning to their original state. "The body's nature is energy and organic in life but in death the body returns to purely an energy state", they said. "If the person who has died in the body does not comprehend the nature of the life and death experience, the energy of the soul can become trapped here on the earth plane and it is here where that which is evil comes into play to trap the mind of the individual in such a way to keep them from reconnecting to their higher selves."

Ted then responded to me saying, "This is very interesting Diane and I am listening". I asked him if he understood what I was saying to him. Ted said, "I do…yet it is not something I have been told before now." I told him that nonetheless it was the truth and that I had seen its' power. I asked him if there was anything that might keep him from moving on to his higher self and if so, what was it.

The Divine had requested that I ask him these things and to listen and carefully and record his answers.

Ted answered, "I am not certain that I can be forgiven for having left Mary Jo Kopechne to die in the waters at Chappaquiddick for I was capable of swimming the channel myself and thus I saved myself. I did not contact the authorities out of fear although I knew that she could die in fact most probably *was* dead. How can I live free when I am responsible for a young girl's life?"

I asked Ted if this was all that he wished to tell me that he thought would keep him from moving on. The reason that this was being done was I had the opportunity to clear his conscience with Divine guidance but in order to do it, we needed to hear what energy was holding him in fear and it would serve to help others in the telling of his story.

"I know that I voted against life when in fact this was not to me to decide who lives and who dies. This is for The Divine to decide. Many lives are lost because I chose *not* to support life and I was a man of great influence. People listened to me." I agreed and told him, "Yes, they did and revered your family." Ted continued, "I was young when I entered office and impressionable. There were those who impressed an agenda on me regardless of my thoughts or opinions, indeed I was not in jail for my deeds because of their influence. Who was I to object to their desires?"

I told Ted that I did not know who these people were that controlled him. He said, "They are a dark, sinister side of American politics, Diane. They want power, authority and most of all *money*. Greed motivates them and fear is what they use to control others. Fear of being without, i.e., without health care in a crisis, fear of enemy invasion, fear of loss, fear even of your neighbor's difference of opinion. Fear is a great motivator. They used fear of exposure to motivate me to do their bidding. Remember, I was young too. I am ashamed of many of the things that I did as a young man, the parties, drinking, drugs, and countless women whom I abused for the sake of the pleasure of the body. Ashamed! How can I move past these feelings of hopelessness and despair over my deeds as a young man?"

"Regardless of whatever experiences you have had here or participated in here on earth, you are capable of returning to your higher self taking with you the truth of what you have learned", I explained. "This truth will educate your higher self and those with you there allowing the greater beings to make changes in the character of man to allow man to choose better what is good and right and just and pure. This is important to the human experience."

I asked Ted if he understood this explanation. Ted responded, "I understand this Diane. Does this mean that I am not accountable for the experiences here? Can I receive absolution? Can I be forgiven?"

"Absolutely", I said. "You can be forgiven. It is profoundly difficult to find love here knowing you may be rejected and also while experiencing many feelings that are nothing like love but we chose the experience nonetheless, therefore when the experience of feeling these other energies in motion, "e-motion" is over, we can go home at the end of life and share the experience with the higher beings who learn from us and perfect in the DNA that which is lacking. This is useful. Do you understand?"

"Yes, I do. It makes sense for what a waste to learn from our mistakes if it does not benefit the human condition," he said. I agreed and then asked Ted if he had any message for loved ones that he desired that I would share. I indicated that I would try to share whatever he asked me to share but sometimes those living do not have the understanding or faith to embrace such things in the loss of a loved one.

"Diane, I have a wife and three children, two boys and a daughter. My wife is the love of my life for she understood my pain and helped me find love in the world. My family was everything to me and if you would tell them that I will miss them terribly and that they must understand that *all* life is precious. Embrace this as I should have while in the body. I see it now. Tell my children that it would please me greatly for them to marry someday and to have children of their own and to encourage this in their own children for this is truly life's greatest joy...the extension of life... giving life to another through one's body. Breathtaking! I was not fortunate enough to experience it with Vickie and it tore us apart though I loved her. Tell my children to watch their p's and q's when speaking of higher matters for they do not yet know all there is to know about these things."

I thanked him for this information to share and asked him what he had learned in all of his years in politics that he would want me to share with the world? "This is indeed a great question and one that I want to answer for you Diane. Tell the world this. Politics though important is not the ends to a means at understanding man's greater essence. Politics serve primarily in today's world as a means of controlling men and depriving them ultimately of greater freedom and the means potentially of achieving their destinies. This is unfortunate for *all* men were created equally with the right to pursue life, liberty and to enjoy the happiness of the body experience. It is the controlling factions of the earth who wish to restrict these activities and to use the energy of men for their personal agendas or merely for greed...and the pursuit of money. The political process ought to protect man's right to explore the body experience. Ideally this is the objective of the Constitution to protect the individual's right to free expression. Sadly, it is under siege right now from factions unseen but not unheard which have risen up in the ranks of the initiated...initiated but not by those in the body, but by those whose desire it is to rule over the hearts of men." He paused.

"Yes, I know and it is frightening", I said. "Is there anything you wish to tell *us*, those of us *here*, to do. What can we do?"

"The darkest hour is yet to come for they will attempt a coup over your nation's political machine. They will want to rule over your elected officials, House, Senate, judiciary, police, and fire, by force and intimidation but know that by resisting the people will persevere and *never* again shall darkness rule in the land. This I can promise you for I can see it from here."

"When can we expect this attempt to take over our country," I asked? "It is imminent...in the course of events taking place in September they will attempt to place blame on conservatives for unruliness and disorder. They will attempt to eliminate free access to travel countrywide. They will require additional documentation in order to permit movement."

The Divine came through at this time indicating that they needed to move Ted on. "Do you have anything else to question him about," they asked me. Yes, I did for The Divine gave me questions to ask him and there was one final question.

"Do you have any regrets about anything about how you conducted yourself in the Senate," I asked. He responded immediately saying, "I regret not telling the entire Senate why I opposed the war in Iraq from the heart. I did not want to participate even by my vote in the killing of one more human life. I did not. One was too much and I had learned my lesson though sadly too late. I wish I could have influenced my constituents with this truth Diane."

"Thank you for sharing this Senator. This is significantly important and I will share it with those who will listen," I told him.

"You have my express permission to do so Diane. I wish you great success."

"Everyone who experiences life here on earth is able to move on after death, to take the truth of their experiences with them, returning to their natural being which is energy. This includes you Senator. Do you believe me? I do *not* judge you."

"I am proud of you Diane for I can see that it was difficult for you to see me as I am now...without malice. I made bad choices. Please forgive me."

"I forgive you," I said and added, "please forgive *me* for judging or criticizing you for your decisions as a Senator influenced many to do the wrong thing, i.e., abortion, gay marriage, abuse of women but I know that you are forgiven and as you let go of all things you can return to your greater self. This is good. This is love. Are you ready now to return to your higher self Senator Kennedy?"

What happened next surprised me as I had not even thought about the answer to his next question when I was asked to assist him. "Will I see Bobby and John there," he asked? Stunned, I responded, "I don't know because I was not involved in their transitions." His response surprised me again. "I can see they are here Diane. They are here. Can you assist them too?" "Right now," I asked? "Why not," he said? I really did not know why not but that I had not been instructed regarding his brothers and needed to consult with The Divine for this is the proper order of things. I told Ted that I would see what The Divine says to me after he goes on. Ted then said, "I appreciate your work Diane. Without it, I could not have let go of the sadness of having taken a life due to my negligence. You have shown me the way home. Peace be with you."

"And also with you," I said. "Give my love to the heavens. Please bless and pray for the peace of America and freedom for her people." I began to cry.

Ted added, "Do not cry Diane. Peace will come by January (but I could not make out the year.)

It will come," he said. "So be it, I receive this truth Ted."

"I am afraid", Ted said.

I then instructed Ted to let go of all fear and any other negative emotion so that he could go to the light in love. I told him that love awaited him and he needed to go with those who would come for him in the light as I sent more light to him.

"I am leaving Diane. Thank you again for assisting me and preparing me to go home. I am free to go thanks to you. Do not fear the events coming for they will not directly affect you but they *will* change your country's future for the better. Fear not. Peace be with you."

"Peace be with you. Go in love."

And he was gone.

Chapter Fourteen

JOHN F. KENNEDY, JR.

Today is the day of Edward Kennedy's funeral and the celebration of his life is taking place publicly. As such, he was on my mind and his last question to me came to mind. I began to wonder whether or not it was the will of The Divine that I assist his two brothers in crossing over for Ted himself told me that they were "there", with him, on the other side but not in the light as it were. I put the question in my mind asking what was the desire of The Divine that I do for it was now a couple of days since Ted Kennedy did go home.

It was given to me to assist Ted's brothers and I was asked to be in my office that evening for the purpose of assisting them. That evening, after doing the usual preparatory things The Divine asked me if I was ready. I did say that I was indeed ready and the heavens said, "We are first going to bring you John. John has suffered much in death as in life but more so in death. This is what you will do. Tell John who you are, a Master Medical Intuitive and Master Healer with an ability to interpret the energy biofields of man with Divine guidance. This allows you to free mankind from negative energy which may "dog them" and keep them from their destinies."

"Tell John that even after death you are able to interpret the condition of man's energy and thus are able to assist in helping individuals to return to their true selves...in heaven. Tell him that regardless of life's past mistakes one can go home for life is a journey and at the end of it *all* may go home for it is in the living of life here that lessons are brought home to teach all of heaven about life's challenges on earth. Now ask him if he is ready to go home now."

Sadly, I did hear John and the first thing he said was, "It is beneath me to go home." I asked him why? He said, "Because I cheated on my wife Jackie beyond measure and there is more. I compromised my integrity as a leader allowing others to control me."

I asked him "How did they control you John?" You may question here why it is that I was calling a previous President, John. It did not even occur to me one way or the other. It came naturally as I was comfortable with the work I was doing.

So he answered me as to how others controlled him saying, "Because they knew what I was doing personally and professionally watching me always and threatening me with exposure. My Catholic background taught me better but holding that much authority gave me a big head and liberties I took I should not have taken Diane."

I asked John who it was that had threatened him. He responded, "You don't want to know for at their core…they are pure evil…wealthy, greedy controlling, and manipulative. They rule the earth with power from this side."

My response to John was that "this is sad". "John, I send love to you and I want you to know that you can go home. Your greater self desires to be reunited with you. You came from God and must return to your divine being. This is the greatest act of love, learning the things of the world but returning to love."

I then asked John if he had any regrets about his time on earth in particular and he indicated this to me. "I regret not being there for my John and Caroline. Will you tell her that she has done well despite the loss of loved ones? She is beautiful and I am proud of her. She need not run for office to uphold the Kennedy name. They will remember her for who she is. I also regret that I was not faithful to Jackie. She was so beautiful and faithful to me. Again, it was fame, money, and then tragedy. I told John that he needed to know that love waits for him now and that he should not believe the dark energy but believe that what I tell him is the truth. I told him that he was able to return home to his higher self which is pure love and that all that he has learned he will take with him and all of heaven will learn from him. I asked him again if he would like to go home.

John then interjected, "I am delighted to hear these things Diane and thank you for assisting my understanding."

I asked again, "So do you know now that you can go home?"

John then said, "I know now that what you say is truth and I believe it. Give my love to the world. Ask America's people to ask what they can do now for their country not what can the country do for them for what country has ever worked for its' people? It is the people themselves who must change the country by remembering that life has challenges but they are intended to shape us not deter us from our destinies. *You* are responsible for following your life path. No one else can do it for you. Therefore, ask what *you* can do for your country and get busy America."

I began to pray for John sending additional light to him and love in preparation for his leaving. I heard him say finally, "I am grateful to you Diane. Please help my brother Bobby. They are here for me now."

The Divine was saying to send John home now as he had suffered enough.

We said goodbye to each other as and John F. Kennedy, Jr. was off to the light of the afterlife.

Chapter Fifteen

Robert Kennedy

It had just been a few minutes of completing the work of assisting John F. Kennedy, Jr. in being released from being trapped on the other side of life, when I was immediately asked to assist his brother, Bobby. The Divine explained, "Bobby too suffered in life. His destiny unfulfilled. He would have done much good but his desire to infiltrate and expose those who were doing great harm in the country was contrary to the will of the world's elite as we told you Diane. They could not allow their hard work to go to waste and so they eliminated the threat. Tell Bobby this and see what he says."

This time all I needed to do was to speak Bobby's name and he was there. I explained the things told to me by The Divine and asked him if he knew this.

"I know this now Diane. Their agenda for world domination was strong even then. They worked hard to control governmental figures like myself and John. I hated their influence and would have exposed them. They knew it so they demonstrated what they were capable of by killing John and then sadly me. Teddy was not as strong for he watched both of his brothers die and he knew they would kill him too thus he drank and womanized. This did not alleviate his pain merely his worry. They were always there to remind him of what they were capable of if he did not play ball."

I asked who these people were and Bobby said, "It is better not to discuss these people. Their control is widespread and they are not interested in being looked into by others."

What Bobby did tell me to speak about were his regrets which were that he did not fulfill his destiny for goodness for the country. He desired honest politics, no hard balling, no lies and deception and murder. He said, "I saw much murder and it continues today Diane. The troops are an example of this. These young men need not die protecting another man's country." He encouraged us to join the fight to bring them home.

I asked Bobby if he had any comments to make to the world for America is being attacked from within her ranks. My question to him was, "Bobby, what must we do as her people?" The Divine encouraged me to ask him telling me that "he knows" the answers.

Bobby then said with much enthusiasm, "*Fight*, fight for the integrity of the Constitution. *Fight* for it to be upheld. This is tyranny you are witnessing and it will *not* end without an uprising. Go to Washington. Demand accountability. Fight the good fight! Demand resignations of Communist leaders whose ideals are contrary to the American ideals. These are my ideas Diane."

I needed to tell Bobby from The Divine then that it was time to go home and to send him in love. The Divine asked me to tell Bobby the following, "We, The Divine, wish to thank you for setting a good example on earth against crime. You were a good man but now it is time to come home." I gave this information to Bobby and I began to explain to Bobby that those who would deliver him out of captivity where there if he was ready to go. I asked Bobby if he understood that he could go and I drew a very plain image on my paper of a heart, his name, and arrows taking him to the light. Funny but he said, "I *see* this. I can go home?" I told him that his greater self would rejoice in gratitude and love upon his arrival.

There would be no judgment, only love. I told him that he was a good man and that I was sending him in love to go in peace. I thanked him for his wisdom for our country.

"It was my pleasure Diane," said Bobby. "I will give you one more comment. Tell the world that life is *not* as it appears to be. The body is an illusion, a representation of the higher self but *not* the higher self. Therefore choose wisely in the body for what one does in the *body* affects the higher being greatly. Therefore live in honor with one's self. Live in peace with others and above all find love and give love abundantly. In peace I leave you. Bobby Kennedy"

This moves me even now as I read his words. His energy was still strong and powerful and moving to me as a healer assisting him. His passion was immeasurable for the love of country. What a loss to America for even now we suffer of the loss of the men who were here to make a difference for America and the world. Each life being a gift and so I thanked Bobby for sharing with me.

"I pray that the world will listen. In peace and in love I send you home Bobby and give my love to all and to my greater being."

"Indeed," said Bobby. "Consider it done that the world may know love, because of you Diane. I am leaving now. Hallelujah."

My final words to Bobby were to "go in peace".

Chapter Sixteen

The Moore Family

On September 11, 2010, an acquaintance of mine asked me to ask The Divine if I might be able to assist with helping her father Allan Moore in crossing over to the light. He had died a couple of years previously but she seemed certain that he was not in the light. She indicated that he was not one to have received information of a spiritual nature when he was living and he had been distant with her. Her father was 93 years old when he died. My friend felt the same way about her mother Zoe for they had not seen eye to eye on many issues and there were many unresolved differences left unresolved between them. My friend, their daughter, asked if I would help them both to cross over into peace. She gave permission for me to share their stories.

I decided to pray about this and the response came back to me from The Divine, "We are going to sanction your assisting them." The time was set for 10 p.m. on the following Saturday night. On that night, I invited my friend's father to come forth by calling to him by name while telling him who I was and what it was that I wanted to speak with him about. I told him that his daughter had concerns about him and whether or not he had crossed to the light.

The Divine came through to me explaining that Allan was attempting to touch my hand. I spoke his name asking, "Are you Allan Moore?" I then heard, "I am Allan Moore, Maria's father. What is it that you want with me?" I told Allan that my name was Diane Freeman. I explained to him that I sometimes help people who do not understand their nature, who do not understand that the body is light and energy when they are in the body in crossing from life to the afterlife when it appears they have not done so. Those who do not comprehend their nature are often trapped unable to go to the light once the body dies and often it is due to their lack of knowledge of who they are and their reasons for being in the world in the first place.

I then asked Allan where he was. His response was, "I don't know. There is no "here" here.

I then said, "Can you describe to me what you see Allan?"

Allan said, "I can tell you that all I see is despair, pain, trouble, sadness, anxiety, desperation, and the like. Most are here because they do *not* know where to go, or how to get there. I am no different. Though I was not a perfect man, I dare say I was not evil. I was just a man with desires in the world like other men. I do not feel that I deserve to be here – in this hell of sorts where souls seek the light only to be tormented by other soul energy seeking revenge on the living. I avoid their entrapment but it is difficult to say the least."

I told Allan t that I wanted to help him. "Maria asked me to help you but she has some questions first." Now this came about because Maria and I discussed the process prior to my doing this on behalf of her father. She is spiritually aware and able to think that it might be beneficial to have answers to some questions she had about her life with her parents and why they behaved in certain ways towards her as a child and later even as an adult. But first, The Divine had asked me to ask Allan if he had seen his wife, Zoe there.

Allan said, "No, for it is common for those commanding others to separate family members from one another to remove any consoling forces from one another. Men are kept in one area and woman in another once their energy is sequestered."

"And children", I asked?

"This is the saddest of all even infant souls are trapped here crying incessantly, inconsolable. It is a tragedy and yet no help comes to us here."

I asked Allan if there was anything else he wished to add asking him how it felt to him personally to be there.

"As I told you," said Allan, "I do not feel as though I did something so evil to warrant being here. I feel lonely, lost, without love and unhappy and I want to go home. I would rather die than stay here one more minute but the soul cannot die."

"Then I will help you go home," I said. "Please answer these questions for Maria who suffers in this world due to things she says her parents did to her. Maria wants you to tell her why you showed favoritism to her brother? Why?"

Allan then told me this story. "My mother was like Maria. She also frightened me with her knowledge of things I did not know nor did I understand. I was happier not knowing but just living in the body without the spirit side manifesting. Maria's strong willed nature was off putting to me in the way my mother's was and I could not relate well to her though I loved her. It was easier to relate to Henry for he did not believe either nor was he interested in such things." Maria had asked me specifically to ask her father why he had willingly given money to her brother Henry, but in Maria's case, her parents would "borrow" money from her only to never give it back to her.

Allan said "Maria was frugal and good with money, not her brother. He was always messing up and needing money. Maria had money to spare and so we allowed her to give back to us as needed. I did not see it as taking it from her but now I see that she viewed it differently. I apologize to my daughter for my lack of concern for her and my inability to demonstrate love for her. She was a kind soul to me. I know now."

I asked Allan if he had visited Maria recently by his spirit for she did tell me about an experience in her dreams where her father came to her and he seemed to want to tell her something. She said that he seemed to be checking on her. She said that she had attempted to hug her father and it was then that he disappeared.

"Yes," said Allan. "I visited her but when she flashed the light, I was unable to stay. My energy was too weak for her light and I had to go though I wished I could have stayed."

I asked Allan why it was that he had been concerned about Maria. He told me, "There is *talk* here about energy escalating on the planet. There is speculation about what that will mean to the living. I wanted to see if she was okay."

"Good," I said, "I will tell her this. Well, Maria loved you…did you love her?" Maria very much needed to know this for her own peace of mind

"Of course I loved her. She was my daughter. I was inept as the father of a daughter who was so full of life and questions about her being. I didn't know how to "be" with her. But I loved her…always."

I promised to tell Maria these things and thanked Allan for sharing with me. I explained to him further about the nature of life here on earth. We are here to experience our energy in a body but when we do not allow emotional energy go or when we are damaged by toxins on the planet from the food or water and we cannot *feel* the emotions anymore, we are unable to be free enough to go when the body dies or when the body's energy becomes too depleted to sustain life in the body any further. But we are all free to home to the light. All can go home.

Allan responded to me that "This is great news Diane for I have longed to feel free and have wanted nothing more than to feel love again."

I shared with Allan about the lies told to us in the world and by those whose desire it is to keep souls in bondage on the "other" side of life so that they cannot go home. I told him that there is no one who is judged by the light. I explained that I could assist in sending him to the light by the power of the light and with the authority of The Divine. I asked him if he would like me to do this for him?

"I would. I want to go home, to be free again. My soul is in agony here. Please help me to go free Diane." he said. "And tell Maria how sorry I am that I did not know who she was. Her beautiful spirit was unrecognizable to me for I was blinded by ignorance of these things. I am so sorry but I *did* love her. I did! And because of her contacting you, I can go home. I see that now Diane. You are good to do this for Maria for I see that she has wounded you too in her anger towards you. Forgive her. She means no harm to you. She is merely lonely and frustrated with the lack of love she feels. Try not to judge her."

"Indeed I will not. I will bless her," I told him. I asked Allan if he understood enough now to move on to the light. I explained to him that he was loved by the Creator and he was awaited by others who wished him to come home.

Allan said, "I am giddy with excitement to go home, to leave this dreary place but I must say that it is sad to leave behind so many. When I get home, we must work on the resolution of how to get these souls home."

I absolutely agreed with Allan saying, "I bless you with this mission. Tell them what it is like and that we need an easier way to bring many home all at once. Please help us to help others who are lost to come home. This is what you can do for Maria and for me as it will clear the planet of much sadness."

"You have my word on this", said Allan. "I will take news of what is happening here with me. Now Hosts of Heaven have come for me and I must go. Again, take my love to Maria, my beautiful girl. She has a lovely soul despite her mother and I. Well done Maria. I am proud of you. See you on the other side. Thank you both. Adieu."

We said goodbye. Next was Maria's mother. Maria had told me stores of how her mother had been very abusive of her. Her mother's name was Zoe and both her parents were immigrants from Russia. They were Jewish Orthodox. Maria said that her mother was mean, abusive towards her, and also forward with the men which Maria brought around to meet her parents. Once Maria became enlightened in her understanding of herself and the world, she says that her mother treated her worse. Maria needed to understand why her mom had been this way to her for it was still causing Maria much sadness and anger in the world today and she was not able to put this anger away. It was affecting all of her relationships and it was deeply rooted in the way in which her parents had treated her when they were still alive.

Maria had spent much time and money in an effort to rid her body of the problems associated with carrying so much anger all of her life to no avail. When life would disappoint her, the anger would rule her being.

I reached out to Zoe in the same manner I used to speak with her husband Allan. I told her to touch my hand to acknowledge that she heard me. I mentioned again that I was a friend of Maria's and that Maria had asked that I do whatever I could to assist her mother in moving on in her spirit to the light. I told her that in order to do that however I needed to have her answers some questions for Maria for Maria was good and did not understand some of the things done to her by her mother. I finally heard Zoe as she was attempting to touch my hands but she said, "I am here Diane. I am trying to touch your hands but I am weak. My energy is low." I told her again that I was Maria's friend and was speaking to her because Maria had asked me to do so. I asked her if she was willing to answer a few questions for Maria's benefit.

"Yes, I will tell you what you wish to know. What does Maria wish to know from me my dear?" I explained again about what it was that had upset and angered Maria about her mother and that these things had caused Maria much pain even now.

"I am so sorry for all that I did to my beautiful daughter", Zoe said. "It was unwarranted and undeserved. Maria to me was an anomaly. I was ill equipped to handle such a precocious and beautiful girl. I was jealous of her abilities *and* she was beautiful. Why couldn't I have had these same qualities? I did not see myself as being as lovely as my daughter so I flaunted what I did have and later tried to fix what I was to become more beautiful, like Maria, my precious daughter."

"Maria has hurt for years over your treatment of her. What else can I tell her," I asked?

"Ask her to forgive me please. If only I had known then, what I know now I could have been a better mother to her. I can see now the hurt I caused her and it is unbearable. If she will forgive me she will be happier on earth and able to move on with her life. There are no acceptable excuses so I merely apologize to her. She deserved better please tell her that her brother is not her responsibility. She must let him live out his life as he chooses. He has long mistreated his sister due to his dad's influence over him in these matters. She must forgive all of us...to be free herself. Then the anger will leave her and life becomes more beautiful. Tell Maria that I can see now with the help of Diane's light. Thank you Diane and thank Maria for sending you."

I asked Zoe to listen to me for forgiveness was already hers to receive for life in the body is an experience we want to have. Toxins in the environment have damaged our energy fields not permitting us to feel and release the emotions which we experience through relationships with one another. We cannot feel in the way we need to feel in order to remain free of negative emotional energy which may remain in our energy fields without our acknowledging them and releasing them. This was the way in which Maria continued to feel anger despite the fact that both of her parents were no longer living in the body. I explained to Zoe that at death we are to take the value of the experiences that we have had in the body with us and share them with the higher beings. In this way, that which is out of order can be looked into and perhaps adjusted in the DNA of those souls still to come. Therefore, no one is judged for the experiences of all are helpful to the human condition. I asked Zoe if she understood and if she was now ready to go home.

"My only regret is leaving the wounded souls of all of these women behind. No one has come for them and yet they too suffer in despair with no hope of going anywhere," said Zoe.

I told her that this was something that The Divine was working on and she should go home and tell the truth of what she had experienced there. "Send us a remedy to move millions of souls to the light at once. Send us the wisdom through those connected to us. Tell us how to do it and we will begin it."

Zoe exclaimed that "This is a marvelous idea and then my life has meaning again. I will go to the light with a purpose to help other women. Give my love to Maria. I miss her though I know she will find it hard to believe. I miss her. She was good and kind to me despite my abuse of her. Tell her of my jealousy. It was my problem not hers to deal with. I apologize and wish to see her free of the pain of what I did to her. Let it go now Maria and you too will be free. I must go now Diane. I see heavenly escorts here to take me. I am overwhelmed with joy. I feel it. Hope is here. Bless you and my beloved daughter Maria for sending you to assist me. I will never forget it."

"God speed Zoe. I send you in love."

"Bye Diane and thank you again," she said and she departed at 12:10 p.m.

There was an additional member of the Moore family yet that Maria had asked me to help. She spoke to me on another occasion after I assisted her parents in moving on. She asked if I thought I could help her grandfather. She told me that he was much more spiritual than her parents had been and that though he seemed to "get it", she did not know whether or not he had gone to the light. His name was Abraham Moore. So it was that on the evening of September 23, 2010, I entered in to inquire after Abraham for my friend Maria. Maria had questions for him as well. She asked me to ask him what he knew if anything about what and where Maria came from and her connection to her grandfather. She had appreciated her grandfather's help when he came to Maria when she was not in a good place in her life and she just wanted out. She said that Abraham seemed to look at her with disdain from the spirit but she felt that he had petitioned for her life in the highest order of The Divine. So she wanted to know what he knew about her reason for coming to earth when she did and why she had the kind of mother and father that she had. Did her grandfather know why her brother was so crazy and whether there was anything which she could do for her brother. I would do my best to ask him these questions.

I made contact with Abraham on that day in September and asked him if he could tell me where he was. His answer to me was, "I am here at the moment Diane."

I told him that I was a friend of Maria's and recently I had assisted both Zoe and Henry in going home to the light. I asked him again if he knew where he was and asked him to describe it for me. It was quiet and so I asked again, "Are you still there? Do you feel my energy?"

Abraham responded then saying, "Yes, I feel your energy." Then he said, "No, I cannot for this is not what I expected at all. I am trapped…like a rat and cannot see my way out. Tell Maria though I sought the light transitioning to it was difficult due to emotional holds on me in this wasteland with oh, so many souls."

I explained to Abraham that I was going to help him if he wished to go home. I asked him if there were different levels there for Maria wished to know the answer to this question. He said, "There is only dark misery, appalling heartache and pain. I cannot overstate it."

"And are there lower karmic energies there," I asked?

"I can only state what I know from my experiences and even then only a limited amount can be revealed. There are millions here. The work you did in releasing the children Diane gave many people hope that they too might be saved. It brought many to tears of gratitude. This brought up our energy levels to feel a positive emotion again. If we could feel love from the world I am certain that we could *all* go home."

"Awesome! I want this for all men, women and children. Let's work on it," I said. "I will help you to go to the light. Maria loved you so much. You helped her when she was hurt. Did you come to her? She says she felt disdain from you. Is this true?"

Abraham said, "She misinterpreted me. I felt regret that I did not stand up for her more. I felt sadness for her miserable state of mind and body and I felt helpless to assist her in any way. Tell Maria I loved her and still do. She was my beautiful granddaughter and very special indeed."

I then asked Abraham some of the questions Maria wanted answers to at this time asking him, "Why did she come to this mother and this father? Do you know?"

He said, "Not really for this is her ascension process of coming to know the truth of her life. I can only speak to my own life. I was a poor boy at first. I knew little of spiritual things. My parents were oblivious of the light of life. I did the best I could on my own to learn but there was little to learn from. No books but the bible and no one to help my understanding. When Maria was precocious and full of lie it excited me to see her but I did not know how to direct her life and her parents rejected her showing her little love sadly. I see she turned out nicely however she should be proud of herself. Her struggle was a difficult one indeed."

I asked him about his side of the family and their spiritual connection. Were they spiritual? He answered, "Not really. My side was *not* spiritual per se. Maria was a fire ball of energy and pushing the limits to acquire knowledge of herself even before she was ready and as a result, she

got burned." Abraham was speaking of a situation that actually happened to Maria when was seeking Divine information, almost demanding information and she had an experience which I do not totally understand as yet. She was physically burned by the energy which came through to her. I think in some ways this was an example to all of us that to be in the presence of the energy which we come from is dangerous to us in our current conditions.

I asked Abraham if there was anything that Maria could do to assist her brother. He told me, "Again, each has his own soulful path to follow. It is not for her to walk it for him as he must search it out on his own. Give him the space to do it in Maria."

"What is happening in the world today Abraham," I asked?

"As usual, Maria asks many questions. I did not hear heavenly sounds on earth and I did not hear anything good here except that the children had gone to the light…many, many children went home Diane. It was a time of rejoicing here despite the hardship."

I also asked Abraham if he had any advice for Maria. He said, "Do not allow worldly emotion to overwhelm you. Take more things in stride. Listen to your friend Diane for she is gentle and kind and has wisdom for you. The world is a place to experience the difference between love and many other emotions. Do not cling to the feeling of those but rather choose love."

"I like this Abraham so much" I said. "Thank you. I will tell Maria. Let the love of light surround you now with peace, joy, hope and certainly forgiveness and the return to your home. I have just one last question. Maria wanted to know if there were different levels there where you are."

"No. It is one dark existence of pain and agony and the loss of love without hope and constant fear from those whose purpose is only to torment us."

Now I asked who they were but I am often cautioned by The Divine not to speak of them or about them though I have been given some insight about who they are. What Abraham said to me I will repeat unless I hear from The Divine that it is not to be revealed. He told me this.

"They are the spirits of lost souls whose purpose in life was not fulfilled. They are filled with envy, lust, hatred, guilt, shame, regret, and all kinds of negativity. Better not to think of them for to do so is to bring their attention." I thanked Abraham for sharing and told him that I would pass on all of this information to his granddaughter. I added, “So your experience is limited to the darkness then?”

“Yes,” he said, “Unfortunately but you can tell others now and hopefully they will stay clear of here.”

I blessed Abraham with love and his freedom. I told him that as they came for him to go into the light and find peace for his soul.

“It is a glorious day Diane,” said Abraham.

I encouraged him one last time to let go of all negative thoughts, all negative memories, and to let his heart be filled with love. I told him to embrace the light of God, the Creator, and to let love fill his heart.

“This is beautiful Diane. I *see* them. I *see* the heavenly hosts,” he said.

I wanted to know what he saw. Abraham described it this way. “Beautiful circular light, almost too brilliant for my eyes. Magnificent! They are here for *me* they say. Thank you and Maria so much.

Thank you. I must go however now for the light draws attention and others cannot yet leave. Help them Diane. You and Maria can do it! Help them!”

I promised to do whatever I could to help the others who are trapped in darkness. I told Abraham to tell the Masters that Maria and I would help with the others when they are ready to send us. Just tell us when.

I finished by saying, “I send you in faith, hope and love Abraham”.

I heard him say, “Adieu”.

Lovely.

It is finished.

Chapter Seventeen

More Stories of Interest

On August 22, 2008, there was a heavenly call to assist my own father in finding his way home to the light. My father had a heart attack one night and he had not recovered. No one had an opportunity to say goodbye to him. What I understood was that I should ask to speak to my father, and when I heard his voice, to ask him if he knew where he was. I proceeded to set up my room and then I asked to speak to my father by name.

Soon I did hear him. I asked him if he knew where he was and he said, "I am not sure. I feel nothing. Wherever I am, I can feel nothing. I am in a place without emotion. There is nothing good here. I can see many people who are without hope. They do not have lives to live, people to care about or places to go. They just are. No one cares about them either."

I asked him what he had been feeling there and what it had been like. I asked him what he had been doing. He responded, "I cannot say. I am not allowed to say for there are those who do not allow this kind of communication."

I asked him if he would like to be reconnected to his greater self for all are able to go home, not just some. I shared with him that the experience of earth is one that was chosen by him and now that it is over, he was able to return home. I asked him if he wanted to return home. He asked, "Is this the truth"? I told him it was, "Yes, absolutely".

I told my dad that I loved him and wanted him to know that I loved him.

"I love you too Diane. I always have even though I was lousy at expressing myself. I love you too. I loved all of my children in different ways. Each was unique. Bobby was intelligent. Clifford too but his gentleness ruled over reason. Beverly was a dynamic personality and very sweet. Diane, you were inquisitive, challenging life to give you more. Carol was quiet and sensitive and a real pretty girl. Barbara was feisty. Kathy, my redhead, was just like me, a great girl. Jimmy was a handsome boy; needing to find himself. Janice was a firecracker and lots of fun. Bonnie had a brilliant mind. I knew she would top them all. I loved all of my kids. I just didn't show them enough. Life became more difficult. Money was harder to come by as expenses grew. I grew a bit despondent I suppose worrying about how to give my kids what they all wanted. I often hid inside my work, Diane. So I appreciated it when you sought me out. No one seemed that interested in me and what I did. My passion was electronics. I tried to share it with my boys but they dismissed me not showing interest."

I knew this and said, "Yes, dad and if they had listened and learned from you, they could have done *so* well in computers."

"Too late now I suppose," Dad added.

I asked him if he knew that Bob had died. I find that many on the "other side" in darkness do not *see* what is happening here nor do they *hear* about others. I believe that it is actually forbidden to share with others. Dad asked me when and how. I told him that it was several years ago from the cancer caused by his drinking alcohol and smoking cigarettes, a lethal combo. Dad asked, "Bob, my son?" Sadly, I had to say "yes".

"This is tragic news. I miss my boys even more so now. I wish I could relive their teenage years. I would have been a different father to them."

"No regrets, we learn from life. You were loved by mom and us, we just feared you in some ways. We were afraid to come close to you."

Dad said, "Yes, I know."

I told him that I loved him again and asked if he could feel my love, the energy of love. He said, "Yes, yes I do. I miss this from your mom. She was good to me even when I did not deserve it." I told dad that I was going to see mom on Sunday. I asked him if I could tell her anything from him.

He said, "Tell her that she was the love of my life, always. I miss her greatly."

I assured him that I would tell my mother although she may not receive it from me as she did not embrace all that I shared with her but I would try. I continued to tell my father the truth that he is free and always has been free. It is the negativity that surrounds him that has made him believe otherwise. He needed to let go of the negative thoughts that he had about himself or his experience on earth and just return to the light and he needed to know this going home when his guides came for him.

He needed to believe that he was able to go home because he was free.

"Do you believe me dad," I asked? He said, "I want to but I have heard differently here. If you have done things that I have done in the world you cannot go home." I responded, "That's a lie. They do not want you to go home but you can. Put those thoughts out of your mind and concentrate on your Creator and that he loves you and always has for you share your Creator's DNA and so do I. If I can go home someday can you today for we all choose badly in this world but it teaches us to choose better and the Creator how to choose better too. We learn and so it is good. I asked him if he could believe that he is free and if he knew when it was that he lost his way in the world. "When did you get off track," I asked?

"I got off track when I became a member of the Masons. This group has some weird belief systems and when I joined them, I pledged to do and be certain things that I was ashamed of and I drank to hide from it."

I asked him what they had made him do.

"Blood rites of initiation, and oaths to uphold their beliefs. Crazy stuff. I felt morally decrepit. I knew it was wrong but I was looking for a place to belong that wasn't church per se where I was uncomfortable with damnation sentiment."

I asked my father when it was that life became so difficult that he opted to *tune it out*? "Do you remember when this occurred?

"Yes, he said. "It was the Masonic Lodge induction ceremonies. I knew It was wrong for me and yet I did it and then I encouraged your mother to join the Eastern Star ladies' groups. No place for a fine woman like your mom to be particularly with her Catholic upbringing and despite their claims of being "do gooders", I was trapped. I signed in blood. They had me." I asked who had him. He responded, "The Masons!" I asked how they had him. My dad said, "Mentally, spiritually and financially. I had to contribute to them to belong and once initiated, you always belong."

I asked my dad if my mother had known that he had to give money to the Masons. He responded that she did not know to the extent that He had to give. He was ashamed to tell her and so he drank.

I told my dad that we forgave him and that we loved him. I asked him if he wanted me to say anything else to mom or to the rest of the family. I shared that mom missed him and that we all did. I told him to forgive himself because I did telling him that I loved him again and blessed him to know himself as love, as light. I said, "Let the Masons blood rites of the Masonic order be broken off my dad by the power of the light and the authority of The Divine. I declare you free because you are free, always were free. It was your mind that was *not* free."

My dad asked me to tell my mother the following, "I am sorry that I did not get to say good-bye, to thank her for all her years of loving me and taking care of me. I was childish at times and reckless and for this I am sorry. Please forgive me. I love her deeply still my Mary Ann. I will never forget her and our brood of ten. Tell her this too Diane. She must listen to you. Life is more than the body and energy is part of our nature and this energy must know where to go in death. It is not for us to remain here on earth but to go to the energy of life from where we came and I see that now Diane. Your light tells the story of light. I will go home as it were and I will see all of you on the other side of life. Cherish one another. Help each other. Forgive each other. Tell my children this. I know that I was not the perfect father. I missed the mark in many ways but I always loved all of you. I had much to learn about helping young people to become successful and when push came to shove, I ran away from my duties. I was overwhelmed by lots of work and little relaxation time, no vacations and I imagined that no one really cared about me so I escaped in alcohol and the Masons and then more alcohol. I was ashamed when I was sober. Forgive me all of you and embrace your lives now while you still have time."

"Clifford and Jimmy, find more fulfilling work that can pay you for your time. You are both capable of so much more." "Kathy, forgive yourself for life's hurts and I love you. Let go of the past and all of the negative thoughts from me or others. Embrace your healing. Love awaits you still. I can see it." "Barbara, you are a great mother to your boys and wife to David. Consider more freedom for yourself. Ask Diane about this."

"Beverly, don't be so hard on yourself. Embrace your distinctive and beautiful nature and love yourself as I do, my first daughter." "Carol, I know that it hurt you when I left you behind one day at the store. I counted all of my kids and thought I had counted right. It was not a deliberate act of omission. I loved you too. Please forgive me. I am sorry about Harry but you are my strong girl and you will find new love but first you must love yourself. Will you do that for me? Love, your dad."

"Janice, let your conscious be your guide as to what is good for Carl. You are a smart girl. Follow your heart. You know within yourself all that he needs for life, so just do it for him and he will flourish. No drugs. They simply add to his health problems."

"Bonnie, exceptional talent. My only advice is to exercise caution with those in government. Their agenda is different than your own as I found out with the Masons. Follow your heart too. Don't second guess yourself. Your "self" knows what is good for you. Listen to it! I wish I had done so."

"I love you and I love all of you my children. Please forgive me for my parenting mistakes. I needed help with finances to help you all succeed and I was afraid to ask for it or get too deeply in debt. I know now that there were options available that I did not exercise but at the time, I was overwhelmed. Look to the best life has to offer you now and let go of the past. Dream your desires and make them happen. I will see you on the other side."

"Diane, thank you my daughter for calling my name and sharing the truth. My guilt and shame overwhelmed me and here I sat, alone, nowhere." "Dad," I said, "Now will you go home to love? Go with those who come for you into the light of love. Embrace your freedom and reunite with Bobby who is there too."

Dad sounded surprised asking, "Bobby," he said, "He is in the light? Are you sure?"

I told him that I had thought so but my dad said, "No, I don't think so Diane. I think he is here, alone as I was." I then said, "Dad, I thought that you were surprised when I told you that he had died."

"I was," he said, "but the light brings truth and awakens the spirit. Now I "see" as you do and Bobby is here."

I told my dad that I would ask how I could also help Bobby then to go home too. I thanked my dad for his words of encouragement to the family members. Dad then said, "I only wish I had encouraged all of you more when you were young. Without direction it is hard to know which way to go, is it not?"

"It is," I responded.

"You are doing well Diane to assist the departed in finding their way home. Keep up the good work.

"Thank you dad," I told him. "I love you dad. Go with them when they come for you, dad. Let all negative thoughts go now and I bless you with love and freedom."

"I am going Diane."

My final words to my father were, "I love you dad". He was gone after that to the light.

I may have been finished with assisting my father but there was more work to do because I learned from speaking with my dad that my brother Bobby was not yet free. I had to help him too and I did not understand the reason that people who were told that if they were baptized and declared Jesus as their Lord and Savior were still finding themselves trapped between life and the afterlife. What was happening in their minds and energy fields that was keeping them from getting there? It was not quite as simple as we all thought but either way, I was not going to allow my brother to remain in a dark, dismal nowhere when I could reach out to him and help him understand his path to the light.

I called my brother's name and then felt tingling on both of my hands as I do when energy is near. I asked if Bobby was there. Funny, at one point in the past, my brother had said to me that he was no longer "Bobby" but was called "Bob" and I should take note of that. I tried but his name from childhood stuck and so it was that I called him Bobby even now.

I told him, "This is your sister Diane. I want to tell you that I love you." I asked him if he knew where he was. I told him the things that The Divine encouraged me to say to him. I heard this. "I don't know where I am Diane. I am here. I am lost. I tried to fight against those who said I was no good but they overwhelmed me. So I am here." When my brother was in the hospital, The Divine had told me to tell my brother, who could no longer speak due to a tracheotomy and tube in his throat, that he must fight against those in the spirit who would come for him and attack him at death accusing him of not being worthy of going home. I tried to tell him. I shared with him even though others around me did not believe. He looked scared to me. I tried to share many more things with him too. At that time, I felt I had to baptize him and attempt to bring forth energy for healing his mind if nothing else. But now I asked my brother if he wanted to go home to "heaven".

Bob said, "Of course. I don't want to be here. There is nothing for me here. No good thing."

I said, "Do you understand who you are? You are a light being having had a body experience. When the body died, it was time to rejoin with your greater self. Time to go home and reunite with your Higher Self. The light tells the truth. You are loved. When you go home, our dad will be there too. I helped him in his understanding and he is being escorted home. Will you go home too so when we return home we will get to see you again, safe, happy and where you are supposed to be, where others love you and await you in the light."

I told Bobby that I had thought that he was already home and asked him what had happened. He told me this.

"Well, Diane as you know, I had cancer. I was hungry and thirsty but they gave me very little food and water. I couldn't swallow whole food and there was no life in the concoction they gave me as "food". I eventually starved to death. My lungs gave out first and without air I was soon gone. I miss my life, seeing the earth's beauty and touching and feeling life. I was without love here for no one talks to me."

I said, "Bobby, I love you, mom loves you, dad too, he told me to tell you that and he told me to tell you that he was sorry. He loved you too. He was just too overwhelmed by all of his kids and trying to support all of us and the Masons took some of his money too. He asked for forgiveness.

If you can let go of all of the negative parts of life, let go of all of your negative thoughts and the lies told to you by those where you are, just let go of any negativity, you can go home. Your guides will come for you and you can go home to love Bob, love. Are you ready to return to a place of love?"

Bob said, "I am. It has been too lonely here. If I had only known what you know I could have avoided it. You must tell the other family members Diane, especially Clifford and Jimmy. Tell them to let go of negative thoughts spoken over them by dad or others and get going. Life is short. Focus on what good they can do. Tell them."

I told him that I would perhaps even that week. I told Bob that I wanted to know that he had gone home but the truth was that in the beginning I was angry at the doctors for not listening and for not taking proper care of him and I was angry at my mom at that time too for she had consented to a DNR, a "do not resuscitate" order which I saw in his folder. I wanted Bob to live. I had to let go of those feelings so I could move on with my own life and now I told Bob that he must let go of all negativity so he could move on. I asked him if he was ready.

Bob said, "No yet. I must wait for them to come for me. I want to say something to mom. Do not feel badly for my death. It was certain to happen as the doctors did not know what to do to help me. Do not blame yourself. All is well with my soul and I am moving on now though I was here between worlds, I am going home."

I heard then to tell Bob, "We are coming for him now," and to tell Bob that they could not wait any longer and so he must prepare his mind now. He was to acknowledge all hurt, pain, regrets, shame, sadness and fear and let it all go. These are energies from the world and they are not a part of who he is and he needed to acknowledge their presence and let them go. I asked Bob if he heard me and I told him that he was an awesome beautiful being of light, full of life, and love and hope were waiting for him. Again I told him, "Love is waiting for you".

Bob said, "Tell Jane I miss her. Tell her the truth Diane. She does not know who she is either. Will you tell her?"

I told him I would find her and tell her to know herself. I told Bob that he was energy and light and love was coming for him. "Let go of all of the negativity now. You have felt those thoughts for too long. Be free now. Are you ready to go home yet?"

Then Bob said to me, "Yes, I am ready. I am sorry that I never paid you back Diane when you lent me money. I was irresponsible with my life." "Bob, I forgive you," I said. "I love you. Let it go. Consider it a gift for all of the birthdays I missed and Christmases too. We had a tough time figuring out our lives didn't we Bob? It wasn't very easy. Forgive yourself. You are good. It is all just about choice in an experience here, an experience of life. Take the good with you and leave the negative behind. Let your mind and soul heal now."

"Thank you Diane", Bob said.

I asked Bob to share with those in the light so that the whole learns from Bob's life. "You can offer much to those watching our lives Bob. Go when they come for you and be happy and rejoice in your freedom."

"Before you go," I asked, "do you know when it was that your life got off track? When did you lose your way in the world?"

Bob said, "When Linda broke my heart. I wanted to marry her and she found someone else. I was devastated, sad and ashamed. Ashamed that I did not go after my dream of aerospace engineering, disappointed in myself and so I drank, did drugs, and lost control of my life. You know the rest."

"Can you forgive yourself now? Do you believe what I have told you Bob?"

He responded, "Yes, I believe you."

"Good, I said!"

Bob then asked me to leave him now and he would go when they came for him. He thanked me for helping him.

I wanted to be certain that he would not suffer the same fate as he did when he died in the hospital in having negativity overwhelm him and so once more I encouraged him to let go of all of the negativity. I told him that he should think of all the good he had in life. Love of a woman, and our mother, and brothers and sisters who loved him. I told him that we all had loved him.

"I know," he said. "It was my despair in losing Linda that misdirected me."

I told him that the despair was a feeling from the earth experience and that he needed to let that go so he would be free. I encouraged him to hang on to the goodness and love. I asked him if he understood.

"Yes, I do Diane. I am ready now. You are a good person to help me. I want to give you a hug."

This was the coolest thing ever. I felt an impression of energy surround me. I could feel it! It swirled around me and pressed in. Very cool indeed!

"Thank you, Bob. I love you. Will you go to the light now when they come for you?"

Finally he said "Yes, they are here Diane, helping me. I have to go. I love you too. Tell mom that I love her and my brothers and sisters. See you there. Bye."

This was the last time that I spoke with the essence that was my brother Bobby. I miss his being on the earth but I know that I will see him in heaven.

******

In January of 2009, my mother became ill and was hospitalized in Virginia. I immediately left my home on January 8, 2009 from the west coast and flew to be there to see her. I was aware that my mother had become a bit bored with life as she was no longer physically able to leave her home or to get about, much less exercise at all. She was finding it difficult even just to get around inside her house to take care of her essential needs. My mother's physical condition left her a prisoner you might say in her own house. She had many health concerns which required attention and yet she could not get out of her house on her own efforts to seek the help that she really needed. In addition I think there was the embarrassment she felt at being so overweight. She had stated that life was not quite as satisfactory to her anymore.

While on the airplane, I felt The Divine guiding me to seek to remote view my mother in the spirit to see how she was doing even as she was lying in the hospital intensive care unit so far away from me still as I traveled. I sought to do this then by closing my eyes and thinking expressly of my mother while seeking to speak with her or to observe her there in the hospital and her condition there. I was told that she had to be intubated and so it was that she was not speaking.

Finally, I felt the essence of my mother and heard the answers to several of my questions. My mother was not doing very well. Her energy told me that she was paralyzed, no movement. She was sorry that she was going to miss her girls. There was a spirit of death there for she did not wish to live anymore in the body. I felt that she wanted my sister to come from Idaho before she would die. She wanted to see her one more time and I felt that I was hearing my mom say to me to please call her.

I then felt my mom speaking to me. She said that the help that I offered her was too late in coming for her. She was too old she said to try again, she was tired of the battle in her body, unhappy with herself and not wanting to start over. She said, "It is not your fault that I would not accept your help but I am thankful that you offered it and perhaps it will still yet help the others you assisted in the family. Do not worry about my soul Diane. I know that I am free to go home now."

I was not even to Virginia yet and I was conversing with my mother. I told her that she must not let even frustration keep her from going to the light when she was ready to go. I told her that these energies of emotion attach to us and try to keep us from going home. I told her not to worry about her sons for we cannot choose for our children.

She said, "I know this Diane. Keep it in mind for your son and his girlfriend for he may choose another woman yet. Though this may hurt you and Dick, it is his choice to make." At a later date, this would actually prove to be true as it happened that my son broke up with his girlfriend just over one year later from mom telling me this by her spirit on the airplane that day.

I said, "Thank you mom. I will remember this. You have a wonderful mind my mother. I wish we could have seen more eye to eye on some issues. I just could not support leaders who steal from others and support abortion and same sex marriage."

My mom said, "These leaders are merely mirroring back to the culture how it is they are choosing for themselves. It is a living breathing organism... life. We create it as we go do we not?" "Indeed," I said but asked her, "How do we overcome the financial crisis we are all in?""Sell my house," she said. "Use the monies to pay off debts you each have." My mother then told me about something that she possessed in her home that she wanted me to have but when I inquired about it later, no one seemed to know where it was or if it even still existed. I let this go later as it was most important just to know that my mother understood that she was free to go home at the end of her life.

"I love you mom and I wish you so much happiness in heaven. I asked her if she would come to visit me before she crossed over. I told her that I wanted to hear something about what she saw on the way. "I do not fear your going mom but I will miss you and sharing our conversations and your love for me and my children."My mom said, "This you will always have my daughter. Your children have given you great joy and now you know why I have cherished *my* children. There is no greater joy in life but to create it and watch love grow through your own. It is marvelous."

"Truer words were never spoken," I said. "Tell God for me that I am doing the best that I can mom. Please ask him for me to help me in getting *Freedom Come* to the people of the United States of America because I have a feeling that we will suffer unless more are awakened. I *need* a blessing, recognition so I can share this truth."

"I will do what I can honey. Who knows what awaits me on the other side. We will see", she said. I sure heard that one comment "we will see" a million times in my life as she would say that to her kids all the time.

"Thank you so much mom! I will see you soon. Wait for me. I will hold your hand when I get to the hospital and I will speak to you. I will tell you that I heard you and ask if it was true that you would give me dad's ring to you."

My mother then told me where I could find it but I have discovered that sometimes people remember a thing slightly different when they are in the spirit. Though my mother had not yet died, I was speaking to her in the spirit. I told my mother that I loved her and that I would miss her terribly. "I wish that you could have seen my children more and their children that they will have someday. They will not have a grandma now on either side of our family."

She also said something that many families today should hear. She said, "They never seemed to want it enough to seek it. It is lost on the newer generations, the connection to extended family. Tragic indeed."

"Perhaps I can restore this if given the chance to have grandchildren through my children," I said. "I will pursue it vigorously."

"I have enjoyed our time together Diane. No regrets! You have done well with your children to show them love. This is all we can do as parents and hope that they too will demonstrate love in the world to others. It is why we came. Why we are here. Tootles! See you soon."

Now do you see the value in my having this "conversation"? When I would arrive in Virginia, there were so many people visiting my mother and attending to her that to have this kind of conversation would have been impossible even *if*, and I do emphasize *if* she had been conscious, which she was not. I am blessed indeed to have this gift as it allowed me a special time with my mother before she would die several days later. And remember, I asked her to visit me once she left the body to tell me things about the experience.

I arrived in Virginia and drove straight to my hotel, dropped off my luggage and headed to the hospital where my mother had been admitted. She was in the intensive care unit. Sadly, the doctors had already chosen to intubate my mother upon her arrival due to her labored breathing. There would be no conscious awareness of my being there. However I do believe that people who are in comas or in a semi-conscious state such as this are still capable of reading your energy and knowing what it is that you are attempting to communicate with them. They can hear you.

I spoke with my mother as if she was awake and listening as did some of my other siblings. Indeed, in some respects, I could say what I wanted to say to my mom and tell her things that she might have objected to while awake for she did not understand many of things which I wanted to share with her.

I knew that it was due to her lack of belief in the truth of who we are that she reacted the way that she did to me. But I had told her about the healing gifts that I possessed and the miracles that I have seen but she merely listened or said that she didn't want to talk about it anymore. Now I had an opportunity to be with her without judgment of who I was and I shared with her telling her how much I loved her. I told her about her family and who was coming to see her. My mother had ten children so she was not without visitors to be sure. People came and went visiting with her while taking turns on different shifts due to the hospital's rules of how many family members may be in the room at the same time.

Sadly, my mother would not come back to consciousness that weekend and the decision was made on Monday to remove the intubation tube to see if mom would be able to breathe on her own again. The doctors felt that this was essential in order to heal her lungs which were full of fluid. My sense was that she would not return to the body particularly in light of what she had "told" me while I was traveling home to see her.

Additionally, and unfortunately, sometimes when a hospital intubates a person, there are risks involved. The intubation interrupts normal automatic breathing and breathing continues with the assistance of the breathing apparatus. The lungs do not always assume the responsibility again of breathing after having it done for them by a machine.

The doctors had met with us prior to removing the intubation tube and warned us of the possibility that she might just go at that time. Honestly, I felt that she would. We were given a time when they would remove the intubation tube and asked to stand by in the waiting area. Very quickly after they removed the tubing, a nurse came to the family saying that our mother was failing and we should come in, all of us, and quickly say our goodbyes. We surrounded her holding her hands and stroking her hair, some prayed and spoke to her. When it was apparent that our mother did take her last breath, I lifted my hands to the heavens and said, "Open the gates. Open the gates for Maryann is coming home." We then sang the song, "Amazing Grace", at least as best we could and said goodbye to our mom. It was then that I felt tingling upon my open palms as my hands were lifted up. I heard in my ears, "I'm *free*. I'm *free*. Tell the others." Of course, in my excitement, I told the others. No one responded.

I don't know who believes that this happened but it does not matter. I know it did and I have been trained in how to have this kind of experience by the best of the best from the other side of life and so it is that my mother left this earth. I stayed a short while and then was on my way home to my own family. It was the afternoon of January 14, 2009, and here I was sitting, on the airplane on my way home to San Diego, with my head leaning against the back of the seat in front of me. I was trying to hide the fact that I was feeling sad and tears were streaming down my face. I had just lost my mother and now I was going to be like my husband, without any living parents left. It was then that I felt the presence of a spirit. I said excitedly, "Mom"? She said, "Yes, I wanted you to know something about my experiences. I am free of the body and experiencing a rush of emotion as I revisit areas of my life here on earth.

Wow! She then said, "I need you to tell my kids do not fight with one another. It is best to settle the dispute about my house by allowing my attorney to resolve the matter. He knows my former wishes. I understand some of you have a desire to see your sister situated there but she would do better in a facility where they can evaluate her needs and address them. Being alone now is not good for her. Her health is not tenable at the moment. Let the will resolve the matter so you all remain close. Life is short. Share your love with one another."

"This is the best gift you have to give in the world in which you live. Tell your sister "C" she need not demand God do something to believe that He exists. To give love one must experience the absence of love and desire something more "C". You deserve love too. Do not deny it for your future is ahead of you still. I know. I can see it from here now as I am on the "other side" of life. Trust Diane. She felt my presence as I left the body. Her heart of love for all of you is pure. The day of my complete assimilation has come. I am going now completing my transition. Tell all of my children that I love them. They were my greatest joy and my greatest achievement.

Thank you, Diane for recording this for me. Do not be sad anymore. Enjoy your time with your husband. I see now how hard he has worked in life and yet his reward eludes him. Tell him his reward is coming. I see it. Do not fear. Keep the house. Sell mine. Pay off your credit card bills and then be frugal while the economy stabilizes. This too is coming. Mark my words. I see it. Know that I am with you always in spirit. Tell my children. Love, Mom."

You can well imagine that I was overjoyed to hear my mother speak of her experiences in such excited tones as I heard them. She was reviewing her life and still able to see what was happening within her family that she left behind. This was good to hear and difficult too. She knew before I did that the family was arguing back in Virginia and perhaps in part it was due to grief and tiredness but then my mother wanted us to reconcile and love each other and to help my sister who had been living with my mom to get the medical or psychological help that she needs.

We are still working on that issue but I pray that this shared experience allows you to believe in the life after death and gives you further understanding of why we came in the first place. Do not delay in speaking to a loved one who is hospitalized and you do not have to "be there" at the hospital to do it. Stop, sit and meditate on the person who is your loved one. Say to them what you want to say in love and assist them in moving on to the afterlife. This can be the greatest gift you ever give to a loved one. Sadly, I would experience another death in my family soon following after my mother.

In March of 2009, I received a very disheartening telephone call from my family. My beloved brother Clifford had suffered a heart attack the night before and had perished. Though I lived far from Clifford, I loved him dearly for his heart was gold and his kindness to others well known. He was a gentle soul only desiring to find love in this world and to give love. He was not married at the time of his death nor did he have any children. Sadly, his only marriage ended in divorce but let this story be worthy of him and may it help others find their way to the afterlife.

I was guided to attempt to assist Clifford in crossing over as it was known that he had not done so and our God told me so. I came into my office on the evening of March 9, 2009 and began the work of seeking my brother to assist him as needed. I prepared my room as usual and then sat down calling his name. The very first words that I heard from my brother were,

"I didn't want to die Diane. I had ideas for the store and a plan with my friend to work for him. I had a plan." This was heart breaking to hear him being enthusiastic about his life but he was no longer alive.

I told my brother that perhaps God had a plan to show other people love. In order for them to see love, God had to remove it and then they would remember love." Cliff said, "Perhaps Diane but I needed love too. Where was my love in the world?"

"I loved you but I just didn't show you enough Cliff. Will you forgive me?"

Cliff said, "Are you kidding me? Of course I will."

"Do you understand what I told you that you must let go of all negative thoughts, worry, fear, money, worries, teeth, let go of them. It doesn't matter now," I said. My brother had struggled so much in life attempting to have success. First in college with the introduction of marijuana, he became distracted and troubled through the use of these drugs and others. He got him off track. He no longer pursued or was even able to concentrate enough on the goals he once had to finish college.

His troubles interfered with his ability to handle life. Though he was a fine, sensitive person, and would never hurt anyone, he could not seem to find true happiness in the world. I continued to tell him that whatever had happened negatively to him in the world, no longer mattered.

"I can see it now Diane. I can see it and you are right. The world is something else…not real…in the sense that I am." Interesting comment isn't it?

"I love you, Clifford. I didn't get to see you enough but I always loved my brother and you were an example for others to remember of love!"

My brother said, "I can hear you Diane and it is apparent that you can hear me. Tell the others that it was Divine will that I leave so all of you would love Jim through his troubles. Love him. He has felt lots of loss already too. His wife and daughter, his youth, and due to poor choices, his ability to do his life's work but he can still demonstrate to those watching that love conquers all. Show him love and he will respond. Can you do that?"

I told him that I could and that I would. I said that as soon as I hung up I would call a store near my brother Jim to send him food. Cliff said, "Good Diane. This is good and send him paper goods for he needs those too." "Always thinking of others, even in death, my beloved brother," I said. "I love you," I told him. "The world will remember you and those who took from you will hopefully learn a lesson. We will miss you so much. Thank you for coming and for your sacrifice. Thank you."

Cliff said, "Here is wisdom Diane for now I see. Sell the camera, the video camera and use that to buy books." He was talking about buying copies of my book Freedom Come to either give away or sell, I am not sure. He added, "Remote view and see it down the road…your success. You shall have it Diane. You go girl. Your success is ahead of you. See it yourself."

"I love you my brother Cliff. Give my love to mom, Bob and dad. Send us love energy here. Pray for us still here. Send us good thoughts. The world needs them."

Cliff then asked me to tell my brother Jim something. "Tell Jim that I am sorry that I did not come back to see him there. I was trying to avoid drinking alcohol. I wanted to show mom that I wouldn't waste my whole life. I was trying to get things back together. In order to do this I had to avoid drinking. As much as Jim did not respect the man I worked for at least he paid me something for my work. I was tired that's all, just tired."

"I know Cliff. You needed more rest and now you will have peace too," I told him.

"You are doing the right thing Diane. I see your book "Freedom Come", on shelves everywhere. Order your books today and sell the camera. Then pay the money towards your credit card. You don't need the camera now. You have Youtube. You will do well. See it as I do. I love my sister Diane. You are so beautiful inside and out. Take care of yourself and your husband and tell your children that *love* is the *most* important thing in this world above all else…is love. Find that here and you have won!"

"Thank you my loving brother. Now do you have the light with you?"

Cliff replied, "I see it…it is coming though not yet here. I will wait for it. I will come to you before I go, may I?"

"YES!! Yes, I would like that…that love would visit me before it goes. Please," I asked him.

"In the night then look for me," Cliff said.

I added, "I love you Clifford, your sweetness will always be with me."

My brother then told me something very special. "Divine is your true name, Diane. Divine, for you are truly connected to Divine authority. Use it well and never for evil. But evil will want to tempt you to use it for their purposes. Watch for it and always follow Divine will."

"Thank you. I love you Clifford." I then drew a happy face on my paper where I was recording our conversation. He said, "I see it. I see the happy face you have written. You will remember me won't you Diane?"

"Yes," I said, "Absolutely! I am sorry that so many bad things happened to you in the world Clifford. All of it."

"This too shall pass," he said. "Life experiences that's all. Lessons learned. Thank you for helping me Diane. This is good work that you do. Don't let a little thing like lack of money for doing your work undermine your belief in yourself. You do good things to set men free. Divine work. Keep it up. Don't ever stop being true to yourself."

I thanked my beloved brother and he said, "I must go now Diane. Some day you will understand why. I will see you later tonight then. Adieu."

"Love you," I said to him as he left and "Go in love and peace Cliff." The Divine then asked me to tell my brother that his soul, his energy had left the body for his heart failed him. They asked me to tell him not to worry for he did accomplish what he came here to accomplish for he demonstrated love under extreme circumstances and despite his own needs he gave all that he had to assist others in need. I was to tell him that he is being remembered already as one who loved greatly but now he must come home. He needed to release all worry, fear, concern for others now, and come home. They said to tell him that his journey here is done now. He did what he came to do which was to show others how to love. They were there and ready to assist him in coming home once he released all of the worries of the world. He was not to worry anymore about money, food or his teeth. I heard, "We are here to take care of him now. Tell him. Send him to Us now."

My brother was on his way to true bliss.

This is truly amazing. For those of you who wondered why my brother was concerned about his teeth, it is because he needed much dental work and did not have the means to pay for it and so he suffered in much pain I can imagine. Not living close to him anymore, I was surprised when I saw him last as his teeth were badly decayed and he needed the help of a dentist who might discount his work to help another. I pray that we will see more of this kind of display of charity in my lifetime for it is difficult to enjoy life when your teeth are hurting and decayed not to mention how difficult it is to work with the public who judges us by how we look. But I will remember my sweet brother for his heart of love for life and others and the world will miss him. Truly, I will.

Chapter Eighteen
INSIGHT FOR THE AFTERLIFE

"Now that you have read the stories of a number of famous people who struggled in death to get to the other side, perhaps you are reconsidering what it is that you know about what happens at death. Is it possible that what you have believed to date is not the exact truth of the matter? Is it possible that those who have power over our belief systems in place in the world have established them for the "soul" purpose of controlling mankind and the energy of life that would otherwise serve them if they were to awaken to their full potential in the body as human beings?

I tell you the truth this is exactly what many of these systems do in spite of what you think. The hierarchy of those systems does not exist in the minor leadership in place in most places of worship. The problem exists in the minds of men who have taken over these positions of leadership in an effort to control the human condition. We are under siege in the world today and it is time for mankind to awaken to his true nature so that he is free not only in life but in death. Life in the body was created to be this way. Mankind was meant to come into the body and attempt to create a life of accomplishment while enjoying the freedom to explore the nature of life here on this planet. It was a beautiful idea and many desired to participate in this journey. Unfortunately, in this case, earth had an enemy of this freedom which has been attempting to rob mankind of his liberty and freedom to exercise his right to choose for himself how to live life in the body. With these types of controls over men which they have established they have been quite successful in usurping the authority that mankind otherwise has to choose for himself how to live his own life.

We, as Creators, are no longer going to allow this usurping of power and authority to continue over the hearts and minds of men."

"We are here to free men so that they can continue the experience of life as it was created to be, i.e., one in which life is enjoyed by all in the manner which they can achieve upon their own efforts and desires to achieve a thing. We are not going to support the taking from others who pursue their destinies only to have government usurp their rewards long before they even can retire and enjoy the fruits of their labors. These days are over and you will begin to see that this is the truth. We, The Divine, are changing the status quo."

"In the days ahead of you, We will bring about some public changes in the leadership of your countries. We are the only ones who know who everyone is and who is serving *what* God if you will. We are more than capable of handling those whose desire it is to destroy the earth experience for everyone except themselves. Unfortunately, they have intertwined themselves throughout cultures on the planet and have hidden themselves quite nicely, but not from Us. We see all, We know all and We are not without a remedy. We are working on this remedy. So what is it that you can do as an average person whose intentions is merely to enjoy life as it was created to be and to explore the planet with the freedom which was given to you by God to do so?

You can prepare for what We are going to do by taking good care of your bodies. Stop polluting them directly yourselves and take action against those who are doing it for you. Insist that the public waters are no longer poisoned by drug companies and chemical companies. Do you doubt Us when We tell you that your waters are being poisoned? If so, take a sampling of it and send it to an independent water testing company and make sure that they are not taking money from billion dollar drug or chemical companies when you do if you want the truth. See for yourselves what is in the water and then do your homework. Find out what those pollutants can do to the cells in your body if ingested or sprayed on the body.

We can tell you some of the things that are happening to you. Fluoride is reducing your ability to think a thing through for it is a mind numbing agent used during war time to placate those who were prisoners of the Germans. Again, this is verifiable. Do your homework. Next, chlorine is a poison. Have you not seen the skull and crossbones on the side of the bottles of bleach which you buy to use in your homes. It is poison. Now why would you put poison directly into the drinking water of millions and send it into their homes where they not only drink it, but shower in it freely because the people think that *government* has their best interests at heart? Ask yourselves these questions for We have wondered for sometime why the people believe the lies of these companies who have poisoned you and your ancestors for long periods of time. Next they would convince you to put a mouthful of fluoride into your children to prevent cavities. How preposterous can they be? The research has been done in New Zealand. Look it up. The North and South islands of New Zealand did the research and took their stands independent of the other. One island chose fluoride and the other chose not to use it."

"The studies came in and the results were that the North Island's children ended up with abscessed gums and deformities in their teeth the fluoride. The dentists themselves did comparative studies and the South Island determined that they did not wish to add fluoride to their drinking water. Did this stop the North Island from continuing to use the fluoride?"

"More than likely, it is being used today despite the truth. This is a sad commentary on life. When there is money to be made, the safety of the people is of no consequence to those who promote and sell these ideas to the public. What are We to do as it is Our promise to allow mankind to make his own choices. When you become convinced even when the research demonstrates that an idea is a bad one to go ahead with it despite the consequences to many, We are without a remedy to stop you. Do you see the dilemma? We cannot allow mankind the freedom to choose and then watch you choose what is destructive to all in the process. We have to correct the situation. It is Our duty as the Creator force that We are to correct what has gone awry in the creative process. This We stand by to do but We are warning you ahead of time that there is some preparatory work to do on your part."

"Make some necessary dietary changes so that when We bring in new energy to support life on the planet you are not harmed by it. Cut back on your intake of sugar, salt, and packaged goods which are without the necessary enzymes needed for digestion and also contain many preservatives which are clogging your arteries and hearts and other organ's tissues. Eliminate as much as possible the use of alcohol for it damages the cell's nucleus making cellular function fail. There is much you do not know about these substances and We must caution you now. Continue as you have to consume them in great quantities and you will suffer in the body as Our higher vibrational energy comes in to the planet."

"Finally, know that the use of animals for food came about when mankind's nature was changed during times of famine on the planet. If mankind had stayed connected to Us during these times, ideas would have been forthcoming to handle the lack of food however in his complacency towards things of the "Spirit", mankind chose to "go it on his own" and as a result, found that the only thing available in their minds to eat were the living, breathing animals on the planet. Though you may find it difficult to "digest" what We are saying to you, if you continue to eat the animals, you will not be able to handle the new energy We are bringing to the planet in the near future. The higher vibration is incompatible with the energy of animals. The two are distinctly unique and incompatible together.

You may test it if you like along the way but you will reach a maximum energy point where if you continue to test it, it will fail and so will your ability to function well. Take this as a gentle warning of things that are coming your way so that you may adjust your minds to the new way of behaving and thinking. Animals are not here to be your food. They were put here to be your companions and to assist you in knowing how to behave in your "tribes" of people. But for the fact that animals have had to adjust too in light of the manhunt against them, they were very compatible with man on the planet. This has changed but We will reinstate the original design on the planet once man's energy is restored in time. You will see. We are rebuilding the planet and with it, the animal kingdom too. This is as it should be."

Summation

The Sum Truth of the Matter

Not knowing a thing does not negate its' value or its' truth. The truth *is* the truth. You are best served by receiving it now so the greater whole can be healed, those living and those departed but not yet gone.

Do you wish to participate in clearing the planet of *all* negativity? Then you must change your mind by embracing the truth. This is first. Next you *must* take action. Begin to visualize those who have departed the body, whether good or evil, and send them love. Tell them that *all* is forgiven. Hold *nothing* back. Forgive and you too shall be forgiven for every person hated knows who it is that hated them. Is this not evil too? Love and do not hate was that not given to you by the religions of the world?

Love! And why love and not hate? Because it is love that can overcome every kind of evil. The energy of love is greater than hate.

This then is Our admonition to you even now as you approach another dimension in time. Love your enemies. Judge not therefore that you may not be judged in the eternal fire that entraps man's mind. Forgive those who hurt you that you may be forgiven. Such is the way of life in the body.

All is energy. Forgive and you shall be forgiven.

Watch therefore for you do not each of you know the exact day or hour of your death so that in time you shall go freely, not bound by the negative energy of the world which attaches to those plagued by their own judgments against others.

One final word I am asked to include here for it is the day of Truth and nothing is able to suppress the Truth at this time.

Eternity belongs to everyone who has originated first with Alejandro for it is His energy which provided the opportunity for each of us to be here in this experience. Who is Alejandro? It is time for this Truth as well. Alejandro is the One who did create this experience and no one is permitted to participate in the game without His express approval. Standards of behavior are given, guidance for the rules of the game that must be followed. When one chooses to ignore the rules of engagement in the game, there are obstacles presented to your moving ahead in the game towards your success and destiny.

Each person arrives here with a destiny designed by them and approved by Alejandro. If you leave the earth without having achieved your destiny this is because you did not stay connected with your Higher Self and Alejandro Himself who is always available to His own to assist and direct and love you through life here on earth. Though it is often difficult in the present times to find time to seek out He who has control over this life, it is an integral part of the process and was meant to keep mankind from encountering the dark side of life to an extent but even this is a teaching tool for when man encounters evil he learns something about the nature of evil however the idea is to remain separate of evil to preserve your soul for eternity in heaven.

Not doing so has cost many their eternal existences for your Higher Being is irrevocably connected to the energy which has the experience of life here on earth in the body. This is a sad and shocking reality which is why Alejandro wants to remain connected to each of us in this world to prevent us making bad choices with eternal consequences. You have my word that there are still many locked in darkness due to their lack of knowledge of who they are and how things work in this world. If every man, woman and child would reach out their hands, their hearts to their departed ancestors we could help clear the earth of wandering souls who are tortured in their minds for their loss of love and life with nowhere to go. Ask Alejandro (God) to assist you in knowing how to help those who are lost, have already died, or otherwise do not understand this reality. Our prayers can move mountains of energy off the planet if we would only believe. We can all help ourselves by helping others.

May the force of His love be with you.

Diane Freeman
Master Healer, Intuitive & Channel for Alejandro -
the Alpha & Omega & Commander of the Intergalactic Forces for Good
Medicalintuitive.diane@gmail.com

Printed in the United States
By Bookmasters